The New Rules of Engagement
Life-work balance and employee commitment

Mike Johnson

Mike Johnson is a consultant, author and Managing Partner of Johnson & Associates Limited, a corporate communications consultancy. The firm's main activities are internal communications strategy, researching and writing on world-of-work issues and management education strategy for major corporations and institutions. He is the author of six previous books including (2000) *Winning the People Wars* and (2002) *Talent Magnet*. He can be contacted through his website, www.mike ⋯⋯⋯⋯ ‌n@compuserve.com.

Dedication

To my son Cameron who resisted visits to 'Daddy's Office', except for bringing the six o'clock *verre du vin*.

The Chartered Institute of Personnel and Development is the leading publisher of books and reports for personnel and training professionals, students, and all those concerned with the effective management and development of people at work. For details of all our titles, please contact the publishing department:

Tel: 020-8263 3387

Fax: 020-8263 3850

E-mail: publish@cipd.co.uk

Published by the Chartered Institute of Personnel and Development,

CIPD House, Camp Road, London, SW19 4UX

The New Rules of Engagement
Life-work balance and employee commitment

Mike Johnson

Chartered Institute of Personnel and Development

First published 2004

© Mike Johnson, 2004

Designed and typeset by Fakenham Photosetting, Fakenham, Norfolk

Printed in Great Britain by The Cromwell Press, Trowbridge, Wiltshire

British Library Cataloguing in Publication Data
A catalogue of this publication is available from the British Library

ISBN 1 84398 072 X

Chartered Institute of Personnel and Development, CIPD House,
Camp Road, London, SW19 4UX
Tel: 020 8971 9000   Fax: 020 8263 3333
E-mail: cipd@cipd.co.uk   Website: www.cipd.co.uk
Incorporated by Royal Charter. Registered Charity No. 1079797
The catalogue of all CIPD titles can be viewed on all the CIPD website:
www.cipd.co.uk/bookstore

Contents

Acknowledgments

Thanks to those who really gave me a great deal of support and encouragement.

Shay McConnon of People First, for helping me clarify my thoughts and letting me 'steal' some of his great ideas. Richard Savage in Brussels for sound advice and counsel based on his own lengthy and successful career 'doing the people thing.' Hanneke Frese at Zurich Financial Services for some great ideas and insights into the minds of today's employee. Vanessa Stebbings of HRGateway.com for constant encouragement and allowing me to use their portal for market research. Nick Winkfield of Stakeholder Studies for letting me use his ideas on internal communications. Stephen Partridge, commissioning editor of CIPD for asking me to do the project in the first place.

I would also like to thank all those who agreed to be interviewed or pass on their ideas, opinions and knowledge. Also to all those people who asked the difficult questions at seminars and conferences that led to yet another line of thought: I don't know who you are, but you helped.

Finally, to my wife Julie for support, encouragement and not asking 'how did it go today?'

Author's note

This is a serious subject. However, I have tackled it in what, I hope, is a fast-paced, narrative style that will carry you along and make learning fun. While it has been necessary to set the scene of how we got into the mess of employee disengagement, I have tried to make this a book that exudes hope and sensible solutions. This is a new style of book from CIPD and I am delighted to be associated with the series and I trust that you, the reader, will be delighted with the result.

Preface

When this book began life as an idea, the subtitle was 'How to regain your employees' trust and commitment.' I soon realised this wasn't going to work too well. Trust, it seemed, had all but vanished everywhere I looked. I am still convinced that this is so. I am further convinced – and I find this a lot more worrying – that many businesses are struggling to find ways to meet effectively employees' needs, or often even begin to understand what they are.

But after much research and a lot of discussion and debate, I am more than convinced that – specifically where the next generation of managers and future business leaders are concerned – we are in the midst of a revolution. Call it the 'me' generation if you like, but that won't change a thing. What is clear is that 20- and 30-year-olds have a completely new game plan for their lives from anything that has ever gone before. Lifestyle rules. Oh, they may work in a dead-end job if it suits another purpose, but that won't last. These people are individualistic, know who they are, what they want and, increasingly, how to get it.

This book is about how we can begin to engage these new-age people in our businesses. The simple solution is to 'let them be themselves' and work around this trend in the most flexible way you can.

I think that their view of life is going to change dramatically how we manage and even redefine what work is all about. For those of us who can change, it can and will be an exciting time of challenge and discovery. For those that can't it will be a stressful, agonising transition. I hope you are on the side of change.

Welcome to the revolution!

Mike Johnson
Little Buckland Farm
Lymington SO41 9HD
United Kingdom
August 2004

Introduction

We don't see things as they are we see things as we are.
Anaïs Nin

The ability to engage employees, to make them want to work with our business, is going to be one of the great organisational battles of the coming 10 years. This book is about that. But before we get started and get you all depressed about how business has done a pretty poor job in the area of engagement in recent years, let's explain something.

Engagement isn't simply a 'nice' thing to do. It isn't soft, touchy-feely stuff at all. There is a considerable body of evidence that points all too clearly to the fact that engaged employees are more productive and far more likely to help your business become a success. Too often in the past the job of engaging employees has been delegated to the human resource professionals because 'that is the type of thing they do – the soft stuff.'

Well we have news for the rest of the organisation. Employee engagement is a hard-nosed proposition that not only shows results but can be measured in costs of recruitment and employee output. Employee engagement is also something that can't succeed by being managed by HR alone. Certainly HR has the skills and tools to assist but it is the line managers who need to know how to engage their people. The central premiss of this book is that employees are increasingly putting themselves (their lifestyle) well ahead of their work. That 'work-life balance' thing is really 'life-work balance' as far as your employees are concerned. To engage employees we have to get a whole lot better at knowing what the people who work for us expect and need from a job.

There is no doubt at all that engaged employees create great companies. As Judith Leary-Joyce showed in *Becoming an Employer of Choice*,[1] great companies outperform the rest. Indeed an investigation by the *Sunday Times*[2] showed that, 'over the past five years, best companies would have earned an investor a compounded annual return

1

Figure 1

PERFORMANCE OF COMPANIES IN *SUNDAY TIMES 100 BEST COMPANIES TO WORK FOR* LIST AGAINST FTSE ALL SHARE AVERAGE

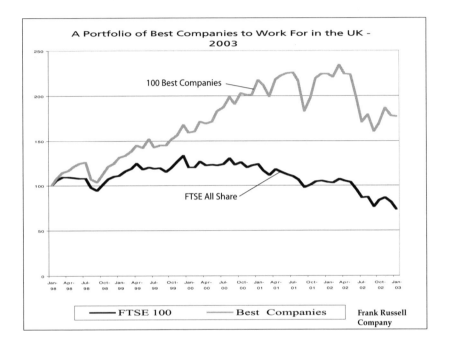

of 12.1 per cent, compared with a 5.8 decline in FTSE All Share index as a whole.'

That's what engaged employees can do for you.

Need more evidence? Management consultants Towers Perrin's annual talent report[3] showed that, based on their research, 'fully two-thirds of highly engaged employees have no plans to leave their current jobs, versus just a third of the moderately engaged – and a mere 12 per cent of the disengaged.' They add, 'thus moving employees from a state of moderate to high engagement makes them almost twice as likely to want to stay with the company and invest discretionary effort.'

The trick, of course, is to make this happen. To play their part HR professionals need to support the line in order to create genuine engagement with their employees. We must understand from the outset though, that this is a two-way proposition. Just dangling what a manager's notion of a great opportunity or a great reward is will not be sufficient. To engage an employee managers have to engage with who they are. You have to treat people as what they themselves see themselves as – individuals with unique needs of their own. If we engage with them, then possibly they will engage with us. My premiss is that we can do that, but before we begin, we need to know just how far we have to go to make it happen.

So we begin by examining the cold, hard reality of where we are now.

Here is a fact, and what this book is all about. People are leaving organisations – large, medium and small (although large corporations are perhaps more vulnerable in the short term) because the place where they work doesn't meet their expectations. In fact employers in the UK, Europe and the US are facing a huge credibility crisis that they have – at best – only half admitted to.

> The real truth is simple: work-life balance isn't working. People – your employees – have come up with a different way of looking at it. It's called life-work balance.

The real truth is simple: work-life balance isn't working. People – your employees – have come up with a different way of looking at it. It's called life-work balance. Life first, work later. And this is what is going to drive the new social contract between employer and employee. This is called the 'I-want-to-be-myself-at-work' syndrome. It is a huge movement (it is taking root right now in your business) and if we don't understand that it underpins the entire rules of engagement process we are going to be highly unsuccessful in hiring and holding people.

'About one out of every six knowledge workers is actively looking for a job,' warns Mathew Levin, the vice-president of Global Human Capital Solutions at the Hudson Highland Group, a global HR consulting firm. He adds, 'Rest assured, that most of these are the top ten per cent of your talent.' Mr Levin is completely on the money. Except for one thing. I think it is more like one in three looking for a job. And it is *always* the smart guys who go first. Because everyone knows where they live – in your place of work. And everyone knows that you have had downturns, and redundancies, and no bonuses and no promotions for two years. And they know that your best and brightest are the softest target in town.

Everywhere you look there is evidence that this life-work equation is being picked up and used by more and more people – people whom we call our employees. But they don't identify themselves that way. They are 'them' first and 'yours' a long way second. And if you can't engage them they won't stay.

'The new generation is more self aware,' explains Norman Walker, until recently the global head of HR for pharmaceutical giant Novartis, and adds, 'they ask more questions and expect more answers.'

He's right too. These employees have their lifestyle way out in front of their workstyle and as the economy ramps up they are going to be off to do what they want to do. I mean, just how many of your employees have been marking time these last years waiting for things to get better before they quit?

This lifestyle over workstyle issue is picked up extremely well by author Herminia Ibarra in her recent book *Working Identity*,[4] 'Working identity is defined by what *we* do, the professional activities that engage us . . . the formative events in our lives and the story that links who we have been and who we will become.'

And it's not just the writers of books who have seen this emerging trend. Everywhere I went researching this book I saw people on the move. Headlines are already appearing in newspapers and magazines that reflect a dawning reality that we are going to have a tough battle and that the rules of engagement have been redrawn.

Here's a headline from the UK's *Guardian* newspaper, 'Solvent thirty somethings turn backs on rat race: almost a million young adults expected to use property boom and technological know-how to build meaningful lives on own terms.'[5]

They were commenting on a study by the Future Laboratory for the Standard Life Bank that discovered that '90 per cent of thirtysomethings feel stifled by the rigours and conventions of corporate life.' The report goes on to say, 'Unlike many of their predecessors they have the means, the mindset and the technological savvy to do something about it.'

Wow! A million of the brightest don't want to work for us. Does that scare you? It should.

'Feeling Unbalanced?' That's a headline in a leading UK women's magazine.[6] It goes on to say, 'If work is taking over your life, it's time to fight back.' The author, Anna Tims, says that, 'There has been a shift in the mood of the nation, especially among women. Our most precious commodity is no longer money but time.'

She's right too. All around us people are saying, 'enough.'

While researching this book I interviewed scores of young employees (mostly in discussion groups in key European cities). Everywhere I went (Amsterdam, Brussels, London, Paris, Zurich) there was one theme, 'I want a meaningful job and I want time to do my own stuff as well.' And these were the best and brightest, the ones who make a nation's wealth. If we don't understand and meet their needs they won't be playing round at our house – at least not for very long.

Another study in the UK, by the leadership charity Common Purpose, reports that almost 60 per cent of those polled felt 'unfulfilled by their careers.' Common Purpose's advice is, 'Employers risk losing out if they do not try to address the growing angst of their brightest thirtysomething talents.' The charity's chief executive Julia Middleton says, 'Let your people grow and not necessarily in your own sandpit.'

And there's another clear, straightforward observation. Mainstream business is not doing much about this state of affairs.

I was sitting in a café in Geneva with a 35-year-old manager whom I have known for some years. Highly ambitious and, when she lived in London, happy to work six-day, 60-hour weeks. Not any more. Recently married and working in Geneva she says she is going to ask her boss if she can work four days a week. If she can't she has a job offer from a competitor that says she can.

This is reality. And it is being played out everywhere there are bright people who want more to their lives than a boring commute and meetings, meetings, meetings.

The next day I was in Zurich in the office of a major insurance firm. The head of business strategy was in a stew. His secretary had just gone to New Zealand and Australia for 'six to nine months.' And before she left she asked him if she could have her job back, *if* she came back at all. Later, I met a consultant just back from a social entrepreneurship seminar at the University of St Gallen. 'One of the big issues of discussion was that everyone wants to work part time and be free to pursue other interests,' he reported.

This is reality too. There is nothing to hold these people. Because even if they like the job they have, even if it does engage them, there are other priorities in the lifestyle that they are playing out. Within this context we have to find ways to engage them, for a while at least. And – as I said earlier – this happens across the board, size or industry don't seem to matter that much. Engage them or lose them seems to be the mantra to apply to today's worker.

The worst part is that we are already losing people – particularly as the economy is widening the options available – because of poor leadership and a real failure to begin to engage the very people who should be on the human equivalent of an endangered species special protection list.

My view is that it is of little good for HR to understand these issues unless they can begin to do something about them at line-management level. If you have good people managers in the line and they 'get' what is happening and understand these emerging needs then you immediately have a competitive advantage because they know their people and who they want to be at work. But if you don't achieve that – and that is the situation in too many companies – you have a problem that needs to be quickly rectified.

Table 1
WHAT PEOPLE AND ORGANISATIONS WANT

People Want To	Organisations Want To
• Enjoy life and work, achieve success and excel at what they do	• Engage the people they serve and enable, encourage and reward outstanding performance
• Do work they care about on their own terms; create and deliver financial and human value	• Provide enriching products and services; create and deliver financial and human value to all the stakeholders with whom they interact
• Create and express a unique professional identity as 'themselves'	• Create and build a distinctive corporate brand
• Find the right organisation and the role that suits them best	• Find the best people and match them to the right roles
• Use their skills, stretch themselves and develop new abilities in their personal and professional lives	• Use the skills of their people, improve effectiveness and drive value growth
• Make a valued and recognised contribution to organisations who understand their lifestyle/ workstyle needs	• Enable and reward contribution to corporate purpose[7]

We have to find ways to renew the social contract before it is too late. Otherwise, all these people with wants and needs and the ability and choice to pursue other careers will do just that. But we can do something about it. And we begin by making an honest assessment of employer and employee wants.

> all in all, organisations and the people they employ really want the same things. So why do we have to make it so difficult for people to do what they naturally want to do anyway: contribute?

As a starting point, consider this. What do organisations and people want to achieve? Are there any common aims for us to build on? In fact there are; we probably just haven't bothered looking at them too closely through years of recession (see Table 1 on p6).

Therefore, you could argue that, all in all, organisations and the people they employ really want the same things. So why do we have to make it so difficult for people to do what they naturally want to do anyway: contribute? Maybe I am being just a little cynical but I think that getting at least some of this stuff right is all about one simple thing: running your business properly. If you happen to find yourself in a firm where the CEO doesn't think he or she is also the senior HR person, don't despair. Well, don't despair as long as someone is taking notice.

And it is the taking notice and realising that something is wrong, that a huge change has already taken place, that is critical. But one way or another this will impact the bottom line of your business. For the better if you recognise it and learn to manage it; for the worse if you don't.

What this book sets out to do is to explain how we got where we are and then try to chart some remedial action: to write the new rules of engagement.

Notes

1 (2004) London: CIPD.

2 *Sunday Times 100 Best Companies to Work For* list, 2003.

3 TOWERS PERRIN (2003) *Working Today: Understanding What Drives Employee Engagement.*

4 (2003) *Working Identity, Unconventional Strategies for Reinventing Your Career*: Harvard Business School Press.

5 *The Guardian* 26 June 2004

6   *Woman & Home* August 2004

7   Adapted from a concept by Tim Coburn of Personal Journeys 2003

Chapter 1

Trust: the thing that went away

The louder he talked of his honour, the faster we counted our spoons.

Ralph Waldo Emerson

The secret of managing is to keep the guys who hate you away from the guys who are undecided.

Casey Stengel

This is a book about trust. Or rather, this is a book about why many employers and employees feel that trust has gone: packed its bags one day and left town for good. If that's true – and many think it is – then what's in the gaping chasm trust left behind when it walked out the door? Is there something else in this post-industrial, knowledge-driven age that is a superior product to trust that can keep us in mindless corporate ecstasy forever?

The simple, short answer to that is No.

No, there isn't a modern-day alternative to trust. True there are hundreds if not thousands of would-be management gurus talking about employee engagement and commitment and new social contracts. But these are just, at best, ephemeral concepts to fill the vacuum trust left behind when it flounced – completely frustrated – out of our lives, somewhere around 5 June 2002 (I can't, of course, be sure of the exact date, but it was somewhere around then). And I, in the course of the research for this book, haven't seen it appear anywhere since.

So what happened? Why did trust pack its bags and leave corporate life forever? And, most importantly perhaps, is there anything we can do about it as far as getting employees to at least take an interest in their organisations again?

Trust's absence from the public and private workplace these last years was not brought about by any single event; it was a gradual process that slowly asphyxiated the foundations of trust that some believe had been with us for generations. In truth, if you talk to any senior (in age) managers you won't find much belief in employee/employer trust. They'll just talk of the bitter times of poor or non-existent industrial relations, when 'us' was the union and 'them' was the management. You didn't hear a lot about trust in the 1960s.

Go back further into any nation's employment history, and you'll soon realise that we may be looking at an imaginary world of kind bosses and cheerful, whistle-while-you-work employees that never really existed. When times were hard people were glad of a job, a living wage. Doing the job had little to do with trust and a great deal to do with fear. Fear of losing that job. Losing the ability to earn and support a family.

A combination of circumstances

So trust had been a tentative visitor to our workplaces at best, but what finally whacked it firmly on the head was a powerful combination of circumstances. Those circumstances have not changed. We have to accept that they are still there and deal with them as best we may.

Trust lost the battle for hearts and minds to a real mixture of circumstances:

- the 'fat-cat' payments scandals
- the 'fatter-than-fat-cat' corporate meltdowns that are still happening and most probably will continue
- the re-invention of the hire-and-fire society
- the export of jobs to emerging economies
- a round of bruising acquisitions, with more due any day now, creating a culture of fear amongst millions of employees worldwide
- the inability – or simple unwillingness – of employers to invest in their people
- the 'realignment' of pension, medical and other benefits
- a total lack of communication skills at top management level: worse still, no listening skills either

- the short tenure of many senior managers, creating instability and inconsistency in thousands of corporations
- the seemingly incredible ability of a large number of organisations to hire talentless people at the top and reward them for failure
- many mid-level executives hired for an extremely narrow niche of expertise and lacking in any type of 'people' skills.

There are more criteria for trust's demise than these, but just how depressed do you want to get? Suffice to say that the list above shows clearly why no one trusts anyone anymore.

But there are two other factors, not in the same type of category, but they seriously affect the way we will manage corporations in the future, and who will be doing the jobs. It is these two that are going to make or break our businesses in the next decade. Deal with them successfully and you might just survive. Get them wrong and your business is history.

The first is simple; too bad that a lot of otherwise bright managers haven't noticed it yet. But they need to *soon*.

Your employees don't believe you!

There are a lot of self-deluded guys and gals out there who think that their staff still believe and trust them. Take it from me, they don't. They may have done so in the past, but they don't anymore. Reason? They have finally worked out the Enigma Code of the employee/employer equation, that in this chaotic, fast-paced world their manager has no more of a clue than they do about what will happen next. So if you as a manager call a meeting and say, 'Things are really looking good, we are on time, on target, under budget,' they know that this optimism can be swept away in a nanosecond. This is especially true of knowledge-based industries where employees are bright, intelligent and able to work stuff out for themselves.

And it gets worse. Because they not only have worked out that you – their beloved manager or supervisor – don't really know what is going on, but also that your boss doesn't either. And that, by extension, can go to the very top of the pile, right up to the chief executive. In this complex world, no one knows quite what will happen next. Your US subsidiary admits a problem with filing its accounts: the share price falls off a cliff and people's jobs with it; there is a hostile bid for the business. Instead of following through on the grand plan, the CEO and his team spend the next six months fighting a rearguard action, while productivity plummets, as everyone speculates for hours on what happens next. And what does happen is never, ever, what you are told. Think about it. Bright employees, those life/work balance exponents I introduced you to in the Introduction (and they are the ones we all claim to want in our businesses) know stuff and they know how to find out stuff. They are way ahead of the official line and are most likely leading the race for the exits and new jobs in a more secure environment.

So, accept right away that in most cases employees don't believe HR professionals who, they assume, never get told anything until it's too late on the spurious grounds of so-called 'confidentiality.' Face up to it, everyone in a society awash with information: working from the basic premiss that there are no secrets anymore is a good, intelligent and practical concept on which to base your decision-making processes.

Being a flexible friend

The second factor is more difficult to pin down, but is equally worrying.

Employees today want more and more flexibility

If *you* can't provide flexibility, smart individuals with that lifestyle expectation will look for someone who can. This is particularly true as the economy warms up and there are increased job opportunities out there and employers vie with each other to hire the best talent.

putting the career first while robustly pursuing the bottom-line is being replaced by putting the family/personal life first while robustly pursuing a better quality of life

But there is a second part to this flexibility issue. An increasing number of employees are opting out of mainstream business altogether. While there may be lots and lots of studies that say workers are toiling longer, there is an increasingly large body of evidence that the toil has taken on new purpose. Indeed, for every report of people working longer and longer hours, there is a counter report saying employees are queuing up at the exits. Look at it this way, putting the career first while robustly pursuing the bottom-line is being replaced by putting the family/personal life first while robustly pursuing a better quality of life. The lifestyle expectation is here to stay and no number of scare stories about jobs moving offshore and an influx of economic migrants is going to change that.

What employers are facing is a massive outbreak of disconnection disease. Rather than worry about how their personal life affects their work, employees today are more concerned with how their work affects their personal life. Any aspect of a job that has a negative impact on their personal life creates potential for personal disconnection. But we as employers demand more and more and so personal disconnection increases.

I am not claiming that every employee is headed for a life – or even wants a life – of milk and honey far away from corporate chaos. What I am saying is that at a certain period in their lives employees may willingly succumb to the corporate life while they build their stake for the future. But, once they have achieved that, other options, that we could only dream of a decade or so ago, are available.

Basically, it all comes down to one thing: *choice*. Until recently most people went to school, graduated, got a job, worked and retired. It just isn't like this anymore. In just a few months while planning this book, I have seen people in all age groups abandon what used to be called a 'safe career' to go and do something completely different. And while only a handful of people used to make that decision, it is now becoming more and more common. Technology has much to do with that. Now, anyone with an armful of cheap[ish] software and hardware can stay in touch and often work from just about anywhere. The office drudge, the five-day-a-week commuter, now knows that you can have your cake and eat it too. Governments are worried about obesity; they should be a lot more worried that the couch potato generation (specifically the smart couch potatoes) have realised that you can live, work and eat in Italy and do your London job on-line. So how do you compete with that?

If we don't make huge efforts to understand the motivations of our employees we will never meet their needs or get the best out of them during their bouts of productive activity.

This is particularly true of the next generations of employees. They are less likely to want a job for life, and don't feel the need for all the security their parents and grandparents built around them. They marry later, they buy houses later, they have children later. They are, essentially, free to go wherever they want. Thing is, they do just that. They have also worked out the deal that their manager or supervisor has about as much information about the future as they have. They saw their parents and grandparents downsized and re-engineered and they are, not surprisingly, totally unimpressed with any corporate newspeak. And they know that the corporate newspeak exists because they've heard all about it from friends and family. They probably have a more colourful word for it too.

In fact the whole working world is totally unimpressed with corporate newspeak and spin. As part of the research for this book, I asked a number of employees (see more details in Chapter 3) what they most disliked about organisations. Top every time was that managers don't 'walk the talk': they say one thing and do another. Also on the list was the fact that they do not communicate well and they do not listen.

So, if you want a condensed version of this book's advice, here's what to do.

- do what you say you are going to do
- tell the truth
- listen to what employees are saying.

My concern is that in this complex corporate world we have created (or have bungled together) it is practically impossible to meet these three, very basic, requirements for a well-managed organisation.

Dramatically shifting expectations

Every time you talk with employees, you'll find that they have very little in common with their senior managers. And I am not just talking about salary and bonus either. The dramatically shifting expectations on the part of employees are seldom addressed in the boardrooms of corporate Britain, America, France or Germany. Those that run our organisations are not fully in tune with the real aspirations of those they employ. This is the break point where the disconnection really begins. But the lack of belief in the corporate cant that is being disseminated (invented by leaders who don't know the full story and wouldn't necessarily believe it if they did) and the need for a fully flexible lifestyle are two time-bombs that will make it very, very difficult for companies to continue to recruit and retain successfully, especially in a talent squeeze (and there's one on its way to your neighbourhood very soon)

Of course we've been really good at disengaging our employees these last years. We've spent millions in consulting fees to find ways to cut our employees' pensions and health benefits (now there's disengagement for you) and then we say we want you to be part of our brand. We've fired thousands of people after mergers and sell-offs and our websites proclaim that one of our goals is to be an employer of choice. We've cut personal and professional development programmes to the bone and then we expect our employees to be up-to-speed and enthusiastic. Somewhere along the line, we lost most of the plot and started a new script. Trouble was we didn't explain that new script too well: or explain it at all. Employees tend on the whole to be a pretty durable lot. However, there is one thing they don't like: SURPRISES! And we are very good at cooking up a couple every week or so.

We shouldn't, therefore, be too surprised when they fail to engage with our plans.

As you will have realised, in most cases I have for the most part been referring to large corporations, with thousands of people in them. Trying to get these giants to dance (as was famously explained some years ago) is a major challenge. But that too shows that any reasonably large business has its work cut out to be a place where people want to work for any length of time.

Survey after survey shows that the preferred workplace today is small and medium enterprises (SMEs) where people say they are listened to, they do get to talk with senior managers and they do get to feel that their contribution counts. However, these organisations too are vulnerable. They are not always the Edens of employment that a casual glance might first suggest. Acquisitions and takeovers pose a constant threat, as do defections of star talent and the financial vulnerability that accompanies many in start-up or stagnant market mode. No one – no matter what category of business – is really free of the concerns of how to engage people. If you are managing in an SME, it is likely you will have less talent, less choice and less room for manoeuvre than bigger rivals. So it is equally important to understand these shifting trends whatever the size of business you are running.

Consider it this way. If you are a 100-person firm and three of your managers – even two – suddenly embark on fulfilling their real lifestyle dreams and want to quit or revise their work level commitment, you've got problems. So thinking that this only happens to big business is a very misguided view.

For this book, the aim is to be able to offer up some ideas of what well-performing companies – large, medium and small – are doing to try and replace the vacuum left by the departure of trust. And I approach the subject through the eyes of managers who need to find successful solutions in order to recruit, reward and retain their employees for at least a reasonable length of time. Well-performing operations work regardless of size or industry, but it is important to realise that it takes a great deal of hard effort to make it happen.

Counting the cost of separation

No one knows just how much a departure can cost, but it varies from three to six months of an employee's annual salary.

But it is worth it, and not just because it can make a difference. It saves money in the longer term. No one knows just how much a departure can cost, but it varies from three to six months of an employee's annual salary. Suffice to say that if you can keep an employee for two years rather than one, you are saving money on replacement costs. More than that, you get a lot more than 100 per cent, as the employee by year two knows more about your business and is naturally more productive. Not surprising that smart companies are beginning to link retention time to the performance bonuses of managers.

But, although it is depressing, we must be sure that the message is unambiguous. Our employees don't trust us, period. To make absolutely certain that all the references to the disappearance of trust in the workplace were correct, I asked my friends Vanessa Stebbings and Barry Wade at the web portal HR Gateway (www.HRGateway.com) to run a survey, asking two questions about trust. The first was aimed at top management. The second at supervisors. While – in keeping with other evidence – the top management results were pretty predictable, those for supervisors were most alarming (I had always subscribed to the idea that people implicitly trusted their supervisor to do their best, even if they didn't really know what was going on).

Not much belief left in the system

Here are the results, based on survey responses from 832 people, mainly from medium-sized firms (who, of course, could well be managers themselves as well as having their own supervisor).

Question one: Do you think employees believe what top management tells them about the future plans and direction of your firm?

Yes 15%	No 80%	Don't know 5%

Question two: Do you think your employees trust their immediate supervisor?

Yes 30%	No 65%	Don't know 5%

This is pretty heady stuff. While top managers can expect little sympathy from the cannon-fodder they daily send over the top into a hail of bullets with no idea where they are or what they are supposed to be doing, the supervisor vote is a lot more shocking. Two-thirds of the respondents don't trust their immediate supervisor. How can you run anything like an efficient organisation if two-thirds of your employees don't trust the person they work for? That more than anything else shows that there is a great deal of work for companies, large and small, across every industry, to do to restore some semblance of respect for those who toil on their behalf.

And if that is not enough, another survey that asked, 'Have you witnessed a decline in employee trust in the last five years?' got a resounding YES out of two-thirds of the respondents. The survey also reported on a question that asked 'Is trust an issue for your firm?' 77 per cent said YES.[1]

These results were mirrored in that most active hire-and-fire economy, the US. A 2003 poll by broadcaster CNN, that came hard on the heels of some of the worst corporate scandals, found that less than 17 per cent of Americans rated business executives highly (down from a score of 25 per cent a year before).[2]

While this might not be surprising in the wake of the publicity that these huge market scams generated, we also need to be careful of judging too harshly. Not every Andersen, Enron, Global Crossing and Parmalat executive had his fingers in the cookie jar. I know for a fact that many executives were horrified by what happened in the companies they worked for. When Shell was exposed overstating its reserves I spoke with several Shell personnel who were overwhelmed that their company – with its great history and great corporate culture – could ever do such a thing. But they were all tainted and one of those I talked to – at least – has already moved on.

And don't for a minute think that it is only giant, global multinationals who are capable of bad practices. Small and medium-sized businesses are too. But as they don't create the same headlines you rarely read of these things outside the local press.

And this is one of the key things employers need to be very clear about. If the employees don't trust you, because you have left a string of unfulfilled promises behind, they are not going to tell you much. They'll act on their own. Little things that employees do can amount to a lot at the end of the day, and can, eventually, cause problems. When you consider that twice as many employees in the US took sick days for personal need in 2003 as in 2002, that sends a very personal, yet collective, message. The message is, 'Hey, I had too many beers last night, don't feel too good. Aw heck, I'll just stay home.' Twice as many? Do you know what that means to an economy? America isn't losing jobs to India and China, it is losing them to apathy.

Interestingly, in the course of the research process, I interviewed an American HR specialist working in Switzerland. She had worked out that, on average, Europeans and Americans actually had the same number of days off a year, except they just organised it differently. The Europeans had Saints Days and government holidays, the Americans just went sick!

Exacting punitive revenge

Yes, people will exact their revenge in ways we wouldn't have thought about even five years ago. And because the morality of business has been tainted by the big fat cats with their hands in the till, this example has been followed by employees. I was in Zurich meeting the head of HR for a very large financial services group, where the CEO had just been fired with a six million Franc golden handshake on the back of bringing the business to the point of bankruptcy. 'The secretaries are stealing the office supplies to take them home for the children, and who can blame them,' he said.

So if business cannot pull itself up by its own bootstraps, no one is going to do it for them. Private enterprise is losing out, big-time. Not only is it losing some of its best and brightest to alternative lifestyles – because it has little idea how to fully engage these people – it is also losing out to the public sector, where salaries are almost on a par, the benefits are definitely better and there seems to be a certain security of tenure.

Anyone reading this in the UK could be forgiven for feeling that this is a rash statement, given the UK government's July 2004 announcement of cutting up to 100,000 civil service jobs. But it isn't at all. Overall, public sector recruitment is still booming and is a safer long-term bet than private enterprise.

The saddest part of all this is that the things that make people engaged in their jobs are no different now than they were 50 years ago. Nothing much has changed, except that technology has allowed us to make mistakes faster and with an awful lot more global impact. Indeed, an initiative called 'A Survey of Trust in the Workplace' by the Philadelphia-based consulting firm Development Dimensions International (DDI) came to the same conclusions that others have before them. It's all really pretty simple and basic common sense. Here are DDI's top five trust-building behaviours of managers and supervisors as voted by over 1,100 employees from 57 US companies.

Trust-building behaviours

- communicates with me openly and honestly, without distorting information
- shows confidence in my abilities by treating me as a skilled, competent associate
- keeps promises and commitments
- listens to and values what I say, even though he or she might not agree
- co-operates with me and looks for ways in which we can help each other.

Now, what do you think the top-ranked five trust-reducing behaviours are?

Trust-busting behaviours

- acts more concerned about his or her own welfare than anything else
- sends mixed messages so that I never know where he or she stands
- avoids taking responsibility for action (passes the buck or drops the ball)
- jumps to conclusions without checking the facts first
- makes excuses or blames others when things don't work out (finger-pointing).

All of this is pretty basic stuff. But we continue, decade after decade, to get it wrong. But now the series of events and circumstances outlined at the beginning of this chapter has coalesced we have a perfect people storm that we have to learn to live with for many years to come.

Just as with the perfect storm, where you can't beat Mother Nature, you can't beat a social movement whose time has come.

A severe shortage of people managers

In some cases surviving post perfect storm will be very difficult indeed, because we find ourselves with a heck of a lot of individuals in key positions who are sadly lacking in people management skills. Unless we can do something about this – FAST – we probably have a crisis on our hands. The reason for a shortage of people skills goes back to the turn of the century (the height of the people wars). Anyone and everyone was getting hired, often for very specific skills and nothing else. As they progressed they were given people responsibilities but not any training or personal development to accompany them. As one wryly observed, 'It is a whole lot easier to spend two days learning new project management software, or two weeks adopting a new strategic thinking model than to undertake the complex exploration of creating engagement and understanding with other human beings.' Absolutely right, there's one thing about people – they're messy to deal with.

In fact that is one of the reasons why trust went away forever. Managers used to manage people. Now 'manager' is just a pejorative word on a business card. It is a fact that if you walk into any MBA class anywhere in the world you will see that less than 10 per cent (and often less than five per cent) of the course has anything to do with people.

Newly-minted MBAs think laptops and spreadsheets and market-share are easier to deal with than complex people. Consequently, in hiring automatons and tech-driven nerds we have lost the ability to people manage.

And yet these are the guys and gals who are supposedly the next generation of top managers. But the other thing that distinguishes them is that they don't *want* to deal with people. People are complicated, they have emotions, they get sick, they have hopes and fears; they might even cry or burn-out. Newly-minted MBAs think laptops and spreadsheets and market-share are easier to deal with than complex people. Consequently, in hiring automatons and tech-driven nerds we have lost the ability to people manage. And with that loss, the ability to inspire, instil respect and the other 'soft' skills.

In this, SMEs are highly vulnerable and need to make sure that they have sufficient people managers – as opposed to 'technical' talent – otherwise an organisation will quickly come under tremendous strain.

Why companies can't engage their employees

It is in that very 'softness' that the problem of not being able really to engage people or gain their interest lies. Our bright, new-age employees with lifestyle firmly planted in front of workstyle are not really being catered for at all. The FutureWork Forum (www.future-workforum.com), an organisational development think tank of leading commentators and practitioners on the future of work in society, says that the five leading root causes of the inability to engage employees are:

- lack of inclusion (they don't know what's going on)
- feelings of deprivation and loss (they feel they are sidelined or see colleagues being axed)
- perceptions of vulnerability (they worry about being fired)
- no positive attachment to a boss or senior figure (often when the boss who hired them moves on, proving the old adage that you join a company but leave a boss)
- history of the employee/employer relationship (can also include perceptions drawn from other employees' experiences).

Although the know-how clearly exists to get employees involved, we still seem unable to treat our employees in the right sort of way. No wonder they don't trust us.

So what happens now? We have lost the trust that may or may not have existed for a few brief hours. Now we have to find ways of encouraging talented people to join and stay with our firms. Engaging employees is a tough task in a multi-choice society, but we have no option but to try. The people wars are upon us again (it will take very little for us all to exhaust the talent available) and then the ability to inspire people will be at a premium.

And I think we have to talk about inspiration. During my interview process I spoke with one senior manager – who ran an executive development business – who told me that the secret of success and ensuring employee engagement was to 'love your employees.' That strikes me as a step too far. People do not come to work to be loved. They come to make a contribution.

So who is going to win the people wars and why? Most important, can you emulate the eventual winners and even effectively compete with them?

I strongly suspect that those organisations that treated their people well in the downturn will be the ones to watch. In that I am personally highly enamoured of Cisco Systems, who – for the first time in their short history – had to create a redundancy programme on a worldwide scale. Cisco described having to let people go as a 'trauma' for the company, but they handled it deftly, working on the one simple premiss of preserving people's dignity. They also realised that the people who were leaving would get other jobs and would be potential customers for the company in their new roles. Equally, they hoped that many would return as the good times rolled by again. The message this sent to the survivors was clear: they worked for a company where people at the top not only cared, but communicated that and lived by it. That is a salutary example of how companies can keep people focused with clear, honest, timely communication *and* actions.

My other favourite example is the work that Rob Kuijpers, the former head of transport and logistics giant DHL, has done to rebuild Belgium's bankrupt national carrier Sabena as SN Brussels Airlines. Kuijpers personally interviewed everyone about to join the new company and then set about creating a giant team atmosphere. Previously scattered around Brussels Airport, he put the entire staff (including pilots and cabin crew ready-rooms) in one building. Pilots and cabin crew eat with marketing, finance and administration and are picked up for their flights by a fleet of mini-buses. The office furniture is a mixture of styles and vintages and no one cares. Kuijpers is constantly on the go (his door has been removed from his glass cubicle) and he meets with all the staff constantly. Prior to Sabena's bankruptcy many of the managers had never even met the directors! Now Kuijpers travels on the crew buses and flies in the cockpit with the crew: 'that way you quickly know if there are concerns or worries'. In 2003 SN Brussels Airlines made the first profit of the Belgian airline for over 20 years. It was all done by engaging the people, providing leadership and showing them the vision and meeting that vision. The only problem today is that despite a wage scale that is low for the industry there is no attrition. 'Everyone loves coming to work here, we're just a big happy family,' he says.

Interestingly enough, Kuijpers did this at DHL where – as a keen soccer player – he created the DHL World Cup. This generated amazing team spirit as DHL employees from virtually every country around the globe competed in regional competitions and then a final in a chosen country (Kuijpers was often known to turn out and play). 'It is all about engaging people and giving them a vision and being very honest in your communications.'

Today at SN Brussels, Kuijpers announced to the unions and the staff the first profit before he went to the press or anyone else. 'They made it happen, they should be the first to know.'

The loyalty and engagement levels that Kuijpers has created were firmly illustrated to me by witnessing a real life example. While I was talking to him, one of SN Brussels' pilots poked his head around the door. 'I just came to say goodbye,' he said to Kuijpers, 'thanks for everything you've done.' This guy was the first pilot to move on to another job elsewhere, but he bothered to seek out the boss to say goodbye. I can't see that happening at Delta, British Airways or Air France. Can you?

Certainly, the charismatic leader who has a vision and the common touch to carry it through helps a lot. It gives people purpose and makes them want to work.

Another telling point is that the boss of SN Brussels sees himself as the chief people officer (so do the heads of companies like Nokia and Cisco), believing that their job is to make sure that the right people are in the right place at the right time. 'HR is a support unit for me,' says Kuijpers, 'my role is to make sure the people part works, that's the critical software in this and every business.'

Kuijpers, of course, is the first to admit that SN Brussels is a medium-sized firm these days. 'You can do this sort of thing with 2,000 people,' he says. 'What it would take to do it with 100,000 I hate to think.'

Trouble is, not all CEOs think that way. Many who have come from finance and legal areas are not well versed in people issues. Being an HR professional in that situation can be tough because it is not always easy to get manpower considerations to the top of the agenda. But if we are to generate new exciting reasons for people to want to be a part of our business and fill the gaping hole left by trust's departure we do need to get top management's attention. Actually that is incorrect. Attention won't do, we need action (very visible action), to underscore and drive home the commitment to build a people-driven business.

Interestingly, the company that probably got it right – and took the emotion out of the transaction as well – was GE under Jack Welch. What he said was 'I am not looking for loyalty, I am just looking for the best 10 years of your career. In return I will give you everything to make you the very best.' Other corporations have tried that and rarely succeeded. What GE watchers say is that what outsiders never realised was the level of commitment that GE made to the promise, the undertaking, to 'prepare you for when you move on.' Everyone knew just where they stood, it was a clear-cut bargain; a well-managed employer/employee contract that no one reneged on.

CEOs must face up to the fact that the credence of corporations is in serious decline (there's no sign of that changing anytime soon). Most smart watchers of the business scene predict yet more financial high jinks in the years to come. Within that climate, trying to get the talent we all need to embrace our businesses wholeheartedly is not an easy task. Without top management showing the way and setting the example it won't work out.

The disinterested employee

we as employers have failed them by not recognising their emerging needs and doing something about it. The danger signals are there if you look.

Employees are scared. Some are angry. More worrying is that a great deal more (the silent working minority) are just downright disinterested, because we as employers have failed them by not recognising their emerging needs and doing something about it. The danger signals are there if you look. This is the beginning of a code red alert. HR has to get the news of this workplace malaise on to the strategic action agenda any way it can and has to have a strong, supportive plan of how to re-engage the workforce. It can't do it by itself.

In the research for this book I was unable to find a single manager who thought trust would return. The best I could get out of anyone was the thought that creating credibility would do just fine. That will certainly work for me. Employees that believe in the credibility of their chosen workplace and a business organisation that fully respects their skills and their contribution. I don't think we can ask much more than that.

In the next chapter we will examine in more detail just where it all went wrong and why, as the wheels came off, most of us stood by the roadside and watched the car crash.

KEY ISSUES

- No trust. Best we can do is try to engage our employees
- Lost trust to a heady combination of circumstances
- Major problem: our employees don't believe us anymore
- Employees want – and will hold out for – more and more flexibility
- Increasing numbers of employees moving out of mainstream business – reducing pool of talent for employers
- More choice of careers also means less reliance on public and private business as a career path
- Today's employees less inclined to take jobs for life
- Counting the cost of departing employees means you can measure the value of any retention strategies
- Part of problems today is shortage of managers who have real people skills
- A history of poor, badly managed communication has compounded growing employee dissatisfaction
- Where CEO is the self-styled 'chief people officer', companies seem to succeed
- There is today a very real danger of creating considerable disinterest about business as a career

---

Notes

1 Survey of 250 HR managers attending the European Human Resources Conference in 2002

2 CEOs and other executives can take comfort from the fact that despite those dismal scores they are not the worst category. Telemarketers at 6 per cent and car salesmen at 5 per cent fared much worse.

Chapter 2

So how much trouble are we in?

There was more misdirected compensation in corporate America in the past five years than in the 100 years before that.

Warren Buffet

During the research for this book I had a great interview with a very smart HR professional called Gayle Weibley. She is head of HR in Right Management Consultants and she has a very colourful turn of phrase at times. What she said to me made me stop and think. She said, 'You know, during this recession we've thrown an awful lot of rocks at our employees. So many', she continued, 'that I imagine they've got a pretty big pile of rocks themselves by now. Thing is, when do they start throwing them back?'

Over the last two or three years I have organised over 50 discussion groups with employees. The objective has been to ask them – off the record – what are their views of their management. The results are astounding. Indeed, it was as a result of some of those discussion groups that the idea of this book first emerged. Your average employee (and I don't care if they work in transport, retail, banking, energy, pharmaceuticals or whatever) in the vast majority of cases does not like his or her boss; doesn't think management has a clear vision and has no long-term plans to stay with their present employer.

Bent bosses, fat cats and wage slaves

How did this happen? Why do people no longer trust, or even like, business? Corporate scandals and executive greed have played a large part. Over recent years there has been a constant stream of senior managers being found with their fingers in the till. The difficulty for busi-nesses' already tarnished reputation is that these people don't look very repentant. When you perform even a brief analysis of the outcome of most of these cases, the number of mistrials and acquittals through lack of evidence conjured up by the million-dollar lawyers makes wrongdo-ing look like a smart thing. As one Wall Street lawyer told me, 'If you've got the money – and these guys have – you can work your way around any legislation, given time.'

We're in a crisis, bring me sushi!
My favourite story of corporate hubris concerns a leading financial services firm in London. Job cuts affecting 3,000 people were announced at 12 noon on a Friday. At one in the afternoon the head of strategic planning's assistant was instructed to take the chauf-feured black Mercedes across town and pick up £400 of sushi (on the company account) as she was having some friends over for dinner. This news travelled the corridors like wildfire and you can imagine the reaction of staff still grieving over 'lost' colleagues. The nice part of this story is that the strategic planner finally got fired too. Sadly she got paid as well.

Of course a few corrupt executives could be written off as the one or two bad apples. Far more damaging has been the growing gulf between the pay and benefits offered to senior management, and the deal available to everyone else. If you recall the heady last years of the 1990s when the dot coms were booming and fuelling other industries too, senior man-agers were in very short supply and firms were offering just about any-thing to just about anyone to come and join them. I remember being in Silicon Valley in California and the then head of recruitment at Oracle saying that if they found someone lying in the street outside their offices 'if he could fog a mirror' they'd hire him. So when it came to hiring senior management the salaries and bonuses became stratos-pheric. What's worse, they weren't even required to do a good job – it became standard practice for board-level managers to be awarded two years' salary even if they were fired for incompetence!

But what was happening while the fat cats at the top were getting richer? Well the economy stalled and down below in the engine room suddenly things weren't quite as much fun. While some companies managed the sudden downturn well, many did not.

For those left behind doing two, or even three, people's work, life wasn't going to get any better anytime soon.

Wholesale redundancies became the order of the day, followed by factory closures and the cutting of all non-essential expenditure.

For those left behind doing two, or even three, people's work, life wasn't going to get any better anytime soon. With levels of trust already at an all-time low and a constant feed of bad corporate news and more financial scandals, many thought that it couldn't get much worse. But it did:

- Training and development vanished.
- Corporate share schemes went underwater.
- Bonuses disappeared.
- The management tinkered with the benefit plans.

Let's look at these a little more closely. It is important to do this, because it places our current position into the real-life context. Because most organisations are at an all-time low as far as company morale is concerned. However, it is useful to remember what many firms did – and are still doing – and to appreciate the uphill fight involved in re-introducing successful employee engagement once again.

Training and development.

Truth to say I know many good quality people who haven't received any kind of personal or professional development in three years. Not a good thing when lifestyle employees see development as one of the keys to career fulfilment. What happened in many firms was that the top performers – the stars – continued to be developed on the theory that 'if we make the top 10 per cent better we can survive.' It might have worked short term but it has left a bitter taste in the mouths of the other 90 per cent. My view – and it is shared by many – is that the majority will vote with their feet when the opportunity arises. Crazy thing is, so will the top 10 per cent. So anyone who adopted that theory is going to lose out, big time.

And then there was the spurious new employment contract, lauded by countless senior managers and business school professors. You will, I have no doubt, recall that before the last recession – when we were in a hiring frenzy – what we said to new recruits was, 'come and join us. We will develop you, we will train you. We will keep you up to speed with the latest developments in your field.' The theory was repeated over and over. In place of trust it was mooted that there was now a new work contract between employer and employee. 'We guarantee to keep you up-to-date, so that when we don't need you there will always be someone who does.' It all fitted so neatly into the theory of the portfolio career. You wouldn't have one job, you'd have many. You would get them because you were being constantly honed to a fine pitch by each employer. And the smart employees went along with this, because it fitted in with their personal lifestyle/workstyle aspirations.

Then it all went horribly wrong. Sure the top people continued to make annual pilgrimages to INSEAD, Ashridge, IMD, Wharton and Harvard (although their summer schools did take a bit of a hit), but the rest, who had signed up for an exciting portfolio career found out all too quickly what a cold bucket of reality splashed all over you feels like. If they did survive the job cuts, they were too busy doing the jobs of their former colleagues to take time out for development. The entire concept of a new social contract for the information age between employer and employee collapsed like the share prices on the stock exchanges of London, New York, Paris and Frankfurt.

But it was still quiet. There wasn't a lot being written about this huge sea change. Main reason? Smart employees in bad times keep their heads down below the parapet. Stick it up to have a look around and you just might attract the attention of the corporate sniper, who's looking for the odd body or two to even up the headcount. Yes, it was very quiet indeed. Those with jobs did them. They didn't enjoy them very much, but they just got on with them. Meanwhile resentment and anger were bubbling just under the surface.

The reason that there is anger and resentment bubbling away under the surface of many corporations is that we lied. Collectively, in the euphoria of the good times, business dealt itself what it thought was a winning hand. 'We are not going to be responsible for your future anymore. No Jim, you manage your own career. But, in return we will give you all the tools you need to be a winner, to stay up-to-date.' It *was* a good idea. The theory was great. But, as I said earlier, perhaps the only company that ever got the whole thing right was GE (and then they only did it for a select group). What went wrong was the economy tanked and there was no money left to do what we said we would do. So we reneged on our side of the deal. We stamped the new social contract for the information age into the ground. Only we didn't tell our new-age workers that did we? It had to slowly dawn on them that things were not working out. Management – collectively – was not delivering on its side of the bargain. They weren't going to keep Jim's skill set up because they couldn't afford to do it any more.

Corporate share schemes went underwater

This is another of those issues guaranteed to store up long-term resentment. Not to go into this in any great detail, but once again management sold the idea to employees that 'owning' a share of the business was a good idea, it was what the free enterprise culture was all about. Now the fact that most of these so-called shares were really options is irrelevant. The stock tanked and so did the investment. Again, employees feel cheated and resentful. It was yet another case of working on the basis that the good times would go on forever. This state of affairs has brought about a huge social churn, the impact of which perhaps has not yet been fully revealed.

Bonuses disappeared

Many compensation plans developed in the heady days of 'hire at any price' frequently had a significant amount of the total consisting of bonus based on individual or team performance. Suffice to say that for many that disappeared too. Now while you can argue that any sensible person would not rely on that bonus to fuel a lifestyle, many did, because no one told them that economic change was lurking around the corner. I was recently on vacation and fell into a conversation with a fellow Brit in a corner café. We were talking about the shortage of tourists in this usually bustling resort. He said one word, 'bonus.' 'What do you mean,' I asked. 'Bonuses,' he replied. 'There aren't any this year. So you make the choice, pay the school fees or go on vacation. I guess we are seeing the result of that choice.' So to add to a checklist of resentment and anger, throw in the bonus – or lack of it – and make life a little harder. Just as we were having to work longer hours too.

The management tinkered with the benefit plans

While most consulting firms the world over were desperately trying to find a new groove to sell to the corporate punters, one sector was having a series of banner years – the actuarial firms were on a roll. Reason? Well, they were earning huge fees in redeveloping the pension, health and other saving plans of the employees of the world's leading businesses. Yes, just as stock plans went underwater, training ground to a halt and the bonus ball failed to drop in the corporate Lotto stakes, top management took another swipe at the employees. Although companies have stated that they just can't be competitive by funding these all-singing, all-dancing benefits for employees, I think we will clearly see some U-turns on this one. As the war for talent hots up, reward structures are going to be a differentiator (they already are in some cases). If a candidate has an offer on the table from you that includes a pension plan that she has to fund herself, and an offer from a rival that is either going to contribute or guarantee some long-term savings plan, who will she go for if other terms and conditions are similar? What may well emerge here – and this will bear close scrutiny over the coming years – is a two- or three-tier system, where companies choose to grant better deals to those they really want to recruit (as a temptation) and for those they want to retain (as golden handcuffs). However, the reason for including the race to cut benefits in our resentment menu, is that it has sent yet another negative 'we don't care' message. So we have yet another reason for this pent up anger and disillusionment. This one cuts deep. If you didn't have it before, you don't miss it. But this feels like something being taken away. It certainly makes many firms less attractive as places to develop long-term careers.

Let the stone throwing commence

I began this chapter with Gayle Weibley's question: 'When will our employees start throwing the rocks we threw at them back at us?' The answer

top management is going to take a lot of lumps and bumps as the employees seek retribution

to that is any time now. And top management is going to take a lot of lumps and bumps as the employees seek retribution.

Next, Chapter 3 is a chance for the employees to have their say about what they think of top management, and what it could do better. Is it an embarrassing catalogue of bungling and incompetence? No, it just tells some real home truths from which it would be advisable for any company to learn.

KEY ISSUES

- CEOs and other top managers don't seem to 'get it': ie their behaviour enrages others and calls business ethics into question.
- Just as trust vanished in the workplace so did development, bonuses, final salary pensions and the share price.
- Companies failed to honour the new-age work contract based on the promise of, 'we will guarantee that you will be employable when we don't need you.'
- Now employee development is being used as a retention tool.

Chapter 3

What employees really think

If thine enemy wrong you, buy each of his children a drum.

Chinese proverb

In order that people may be happy in their work, these three things are needed: They must be for it. They must not do too much of it. And they must have a sense of success in it.

John Ruskin

So what do employees really think about the way they are treated at work? Is there some kind of corporate Utopia out there, where kind managers smile benignly on their people, all the while showering them with bonuses and other perks? Well, not really. However, it has to be said that there are some firms that are standouts in the 'best employer' category. I asked a cross-section of (mainly HR) management professionals in small-, medium- and large-sized firms for their frank views. This is the result. What is most significant is that although these views are drawn from the UK, the rest of Europe and the US, they all have a remarkable similarity. Indeed, a theme around engagement and communication ran through all the interviews. These views are coming from practising professionals, who have probably seen most of what corporate life can throw at them. It doesn't matter about fancy theories, this is telling it like it is and it will pay us to heed their message. Remember too as you read this, that all these people are themselves managers. They may not be at the very peak of the corporation, but they do lead teams and divisions and groups. They are commenting on what they see. These are, in most cases, the horses of the business that pull it along. What they most need to know is which way to pull. If top management cannot point out the route and give a compelling vision of why we want to go there, these managers cannot do their jobs. You can have every employee survey under the sun, but if you don't heed these general comments and have a plan to act on them, you will never ever really get to grips with engaging your employees. And that is what we must all set out to do if we want our businesses to succeed.

Sheila Bates is an HR professional with Rockwell Automation's European headquarters in Belgium.

Mike Johnson: What do you think – based on your own experiences – are the best ways to create engagement and commitment at work?

SB: Be honest and open. Tell it as it really is. Walk the talk and be consistent. Take the tough decisions when you have to. I am heartily sick of weak leaders.

MJ: What do you think – based on your own experiences – are the biggest turn-offs to employee engagement and commitment at work?

SB: Telling your people they are the most important asset for the business: 99.99 per cent of companies then behave in the opposite manner. Failure to manage the void between saying and doing.

MJ: Which company (or companies) do you most admire in the way they engage and motivate employees?

SB: I still think that Orange is a shining example, because they are still committed to the growth and development of their staff, even in the current climate.

MJ: If you were CEO for the day, what would be the one thing you would do to improve levels of engagement and commitment in your business?

SB: Wave a magic wand and ensure that all managers never ever again made crappy comments to staff that they were never going to be able to deliver on.

The questions that follow have been edited to avoid repetition.

Jackie Alexander is director of HR, Europe, for Novell/Cambridge

Technologies, a medium-sized, globally active software firm, at their Paris headquarters.

MJ: What are the best ways to create engagement?

JA: Transparent objectives, clear goals and well-articulated responsibilities with the appropriate level of accountability attached.

MJ: What are the biggest turn-offs to employee engagement?

JA: Where compensation and reward is not perceived/does not correspond to effort of individuals.

Where corporate management says one thing and then implements a process that drives totally different behaviours. Example: 'We need to work as a team', then pays for individual contribution only.

Where clear promises are made and then reneged on – usually because management isn't courageous enough to tell the truth about the challenges facing the business. Then is unable to meet its commitments because 'there's no money', 'we missed our targets', 'the Euro / Dollar exchange rate shifted.'

MJ: Which company do you most admire?

JA: Don't think I have any clear favourites as all companies seem to be struggling with the evolving paradigm of what employment really means these days. Therefore, I think that excellence in managing people is only partially based on having strong processes for developing and rewarding people. What really counts is how strongly employees are engaged in the day-to-day struggle of the business and can therefore evaluate for themselves how they and the company are doing. But if I had to choose a company it would be Cisco for its slick integration processes after acquisitions (boot-camps, heavy communication efforts). I also rate IBM, simply because you hear people say it is still a great place to work.

Leslie Raymond is an assistant vice-president and HR business partner, international operations, at the global headquarters of insurance firm Winterthur in Switzerland.

MJ: What are the best ways to create engagement?

LR: Open and candid communications at all levels. No favouritism, everyone treated the same way.

MJ: What are the biggest turn-offs to employee engagement?

LR: Realising that you are the last to know what is going on in the company. No communication on why and how the company handles controversial issues.

MJ: Which company do you most admire?

LR: Kraft Food and Philip Morris. Both have strong cultures and employees take pride in working there. There is also a consistent message from the CEO.

MJ: If you were CEO for the day, what would be the one thing you would do?

LR: I would speak to as many people as possible to create an open climate of trust and engagement.

Anne Chivers is head of learning an organisational development at the Housing Corporation in London.

MJ: What are the best ways to create engagement?

AC: Communicate, communicate, communicate. Treat employees with trust and respect. Provide opportunities to learn and grow. Share your strategies and invite ideas. Reward effort and deal quickly with the incompetent.

MJ: What are the biggest turn-offs to employee engagement?

AC: Lack of recognition. Incompetent managers. Rewarding the wrong people. Bullying. Greed.

MJ: Which company do you most admire?

AC: Microsoft: they know that their survival depends on attracting and retaining the talent they need.

MJ: If you were CEO for the day, what would be the one thing you would do?

AC: Get out there and meet the employees and listen to what they have to say.

Jackie Van Aubel is the founder and president of Sponsart, a boutique consulting firm that advises major firms in sponsoring cultural events all over the world. She lives and works in Monte Carlo.

MJ: What are the best ways to create engagement?

JVA: Make sure that the company has a culture and that top management makes sure everyone is in line with that culture. Top management must communicate and walk the talk. Have respect for all employees; give chances, be open and transparent.

MJ: What are the biggest turn-offs to employee engagement?

JVA: Selling off well-performing units to generate cash for other business. This is perceived as being 'punished' for doing well. It demotivates employees and everyone starts working for themselves and their own interests; so no one goes the extra mile.

MJ: If you were CEO for the day, what would be the one thing you would do?

JVA: Realise that I should be in business for the business to continue to exist. If that is not the case, be transparent from day one, and say so. Walk the talk and realise that the bottom-line is not all that must be taken into consideration for decisions and strategies. Hire more women. They often prove more straightforward, act less like political animals and are more outspoken.

Clemens Reisbeck is head of talent management at Barclays Capital in London.

MJ: What are the best ways to create engagement?

CR: The key for trust and commitment to develop and flourish are open, clear and honest communication. However, the first thing is to trust your employees. You need to trust your people first, before they start trusting you.

MJ: What are the biggest turn-offs to employee engagement?

CR: Not trusting. Not walking the talk. Unclear expectations, responsibilities and communication. Not keeping the promises made in hiring the person into the firm.

MJ: Which company do you most admire?

CR: To be honest, based on my own experiences I don't know of an organisation I would admire for their way of motivating and engaging their employees. However, I would think that organisations with these qualities are more often found among small to mid-sized companies, or start-ups where you have a leader figure. I think these kinds of organisations have a high degree of overlap between company interests and values and the values and interests of the employees.

MJ: If you were CEO for the day, what would be the one thing you would do?

CR: Ask employees, 'What do I need to STOP doing that destroys your commitment and trust?' Then act on it. Make sure you have clear, open and honest communication. The people working for you are not dumb!

Don Bates is managing director of Media Distribution Services, America's largest PR media, mailing, printing, fax and e-mail service. He lives and works in Manhattan.

MJ: What are the best ways to create engagement?

DB: First, talk to ALL your employees. Have an internal communications programme, no matter how modest, that addresses the big picture issues and that attempts to instil camaraderie. In your actual communications, be as direct and candid as you can be without stimulating upset and animosity. Minimise the scuttlebutt and what employees learn via the rumour mill.

MJ: What are the biggest turn-offs to employee?

DB: Not talking to them. Not involving them in decision-making that affects their performance and success. Not being candid or fair.

MJ: Which company do you most admire?

DB: The obvious example would be one of the big corporations that pay the best, offer the most opportunities and communicate the most on internal matters. In reality, I admire any company large or small that do these things as best they can within their particular limitations. Using excuses such as 'we're too small' or 'we don't have the resources,' isn't admirable and it is counter-productive to almost every measure of serious business success.

MJ: If you were CEO for the day, what would be the one thing you would do?

DB: Ask my top managers to tell me what their goals are for improving their performance and their staff's performance over the next year in relation to the company's most pressing needs. Then I would help them refine those goals into a reasonable commitment that I would use to judge their success or failure. I would put some feet to the fire, but commit to supporting them in not getting burned.

Clem Cheng is vice-president HR for Cigna Insurance at their head-quarters in Philadelphia.

MJ: What are the best ways to create engagement and commitment at work?

CC: Effective leadership that sets a strong direction for the enterprise. Communicating with honesty. Involving employees at all levels and establishing appropriate rewards.

I also believe that to generate real commitment there has to be an appropriate level of passion about the mission and work. However, this does not have to be some high calling. I have seen organisations that get employees passionate about relatively basic work such as retailing or food service. It is all about *how* you do it.

MJ: What are the biggest turn-offs to employee engagement and commitment at work?

CC: Management that does not walk the talk, especially leaders who say one thing and do not model the behaviours. Also excessive greed, over-the-top executive perks and arrogance are just huge turn-offs. A lack of focus on the customer is also a good way to introduce cynicism.

MJ: Which company do you most admire?

CC: W.L. Gore and Associates (the manufacturers of Gore-Tex fabric, and voted best company to work for in the UK in 2003 by a *Sunday Times* poll): for their organic culture, concept of natural leadership (leaders are not appointed, but emerge) and high involvement work environment. Southwest Airlines: unique culture and clear track record of successful performance. Nordstrom's: equip and empower employees to truly help the customer.

MJ: If you were CEO for the day, what would be the one thing you would do?

CC: Be visible with employees at all levels. Lead with my heart in addition to my head. Speak with candour and optimism but also make the tough calls about how to get the desired level of performance.

John Jeffcock is the founder and managing director of Winmark, a London-based market research firm that specialises in employee research.

MJ: What are the best ways to create engagement and commitment at work?

JJ: I think you need to invest in the person, not just the employee. What I mean by this is that the company needs to demonstrate it cares outside of the normal requirements. That is, break the rules in the employee's favour.

MJ: If you were CEO for the day, what would be the one thing you would do?

JJ: What I would do is identify, say, 10 special cases (people in a hard place or difficult circumstances) at a local level and then do something above and beyond the call of duty.

Gayle Weibley is executive vice-president HR for Right Management Consulting, based in their world headquarters in Philadelphia.

MJ: What are the best ways to create engagement?

GW: For me, and from what I hear from employees everywhere I have worked, people place highest on their list the credibility factor. Leaders engender trust and commitment when they demonstrate core values that are trustworthy, and show that they are willing to move heaven and earth to keep them. I believe that people will quickly follow in behind someone who is genuine, authentic, honest and respects others. This may sound over-simplistic and trite, but the problem is that a heck of a lot of executives are just not that honest and people know it.

MJ: What are the biggest turn-offs to employee engagement?

GW: I don't see many business leaders who check their egos at the door. Most people seem to be always working an 'angle' or an 'agenda' that will ultimately benefit them individually and people see through that. At Right, we operate on a simple rule: demonstrate, don't declare.

MJ: If you were CEO for the day, what would be the one thing you would do?

GW: If I was CEO for a day in a company where these problems existed, I would probably clean house. Then I would immediately follow up with a videoconference to the entire company explaining the 'new platform'. Then I would surround myself with people who had a track record of demonstrating the appropriate behaviours and financial success for their companies.

Pam Hurst is the founder of Heart of the Business, a small, UK-based HR consultancy.

MJ: What are the best ways to create engagement?

PH: Plain and simple – involvement. Treat all employees as responsible adults who want to contribute to the success of the company. All employees are capable of understanding the big picture and acting on it if it is communicated to them.

MJ: What are the biggest turn-offs to employee engagement?

PH: Not being treated as adults (see above). Being given explicit or implicit messages (not always deliberate) that 'you're not being paid to think.' Mixed messages like top management spouting stuff about 'people being our most important asset,' and then springing change programmes with job changes or losses, that have been hatched in secret. That really does mess up the trust relationship. Worse still it takes ages to rebuild once it is lost.

By the way, one of the best ways to turn employees off is a badly managed appraisal system – and there are plenty about. I am a great fan of a good appraisal system, but they have to be simple, in the control of the employee and integrated into the company's strategic business planning and performance management. Otherwise they just won't be effective over the long term.

MJ: What company do you most admire?

PH: Given its size I think Tesco does a pretty good job with employee initiatives. I also like the sound of what the Savoy hotel group have been doing in people management.

MJ: If you were CEO for the day, what would be the one thing you would do?

PH: I would appoint me to review, improve and/or implement a really sound corporate and individual performance management approach and process. That *is* a serious proposition! Equally, if I only had a day, as CEO I could do some really stirring hearts and minds stuff, which could engender trust and commitment (as long as I hadn't previously blown it!). But, frankly it would be what I and my management team did subsequently that would be the real test of ongoing trust and commitment.

Currently based in Brussels, **Bill Bauer** is senior manager international accounts with Vodafone.

MJ: What are the best ways to create engagement?

BB: I think that stability is all too often overlooked. But people need a certain level of stability in the messages that they get from management in order to commit their full energies.

Consistency between message and action. People want to see that pronouncements of management are matched by their actions.

People need an opportunity to learn and develop, this doesn't just mean formal training either. It means the chance to spend time with respected colleagues (inside and outside the firm), try new things, get great coaching and so on.

People need to have a coherence between responsibility, resources and rewards, knowing just how these fit together – and I don't mean just monetary rewards either.

My view is that people don't work for companies, they work for people. A colleague of mine once said, '90 per cent of every job is your boss.' And I think we need to recognise that an employee's line manager is critical to that person's performance and whether they stay or go. Personally, I think one of the most toxic by-products of the Internet 90s was a disdain for the role of line management.

MJ: What are the biggest turn-offs to employee engagement?

BB: Instability: 'This is the year we crack the Enterprise Market.' Yep, we're going to focus on it for a whole 90 days – then try something else.

Inconsistency: 'All employees must travel Economy class' – unless you senior enough to have your PA instruct the travel agency otherwise.

Opportunity: 'You've done a great job this year,' So stay in your box and do it again. And again. And again.

MJ: What company do you most admire?

BB: Most of the companies I have worked for in my career have, frankly done a pretty poor job in this area. And I certainly don't see much improvement.

MJ: If you were CEO for the day, what would be the one thing you would do?

BB: Forcing every director to look out for stars all the time, in the knowledge that this was going to be constantly reviewed.

Forcing them to tackle the poor performers who subtract value – the 'anchor draggers', who make everyone's working life worse. It is a critically important (if uncomfortable) leadership role.

Ensuring that appraisal processes are thoroughly and consistently implemented.

Challenging directors to think seriously about the kind of behaviours that are rewarded – as opposed to the kind of behaviour they are asking for.

Clearly putting the onus for nurturing talent and addressing poor performance at the door of line management – not HR.

Communicating the message that people and leadership matter – by example rather than by slogans.

Extreme motivation

I also asked some of the professionals I interviewed for any 'war' stories concerning what I termed, 'extreme examples of employee motivation.' Wherever you go in the world of business you will always find the sublime, closely followed by the downright ridiculous.

Off with his head!

Ann Chivers of the Housing Corporation in London recalled this bizarre practice. 'Annually firing the bottom 10 per cent of performers, without regard to coaching, development or examining recruitment and selection processes and those that hired them (or why these people were hired in the first place). The concept is that those who survived the annual cull would be motivated to work even harder.' What a great way to build a talent culture!

Don't give me the bonus, but I'll keep the jet

Don Bates of Manhattan-based Media Distribution Services says that his favourite extreme motivation story involves that maverick of the multinationals, Jack Welch. Bates says: 'When GE offered him – at age 63 – a $100 million pay package to stay with them until he was 65 – and he turned it down!' Here's what happened. In 1996 Welch was 61 years old and he had just had major heart surgery. All his predecessors had retired at around 62 and 63. The board offered him $100 million in restricted stock to stay until he was 65. Welch said he didn't want the money but what he did want was to keep the company plane that was at his disposal and the company apartment in New York, which cost GE about $1.7 million a year.

A first day experience

Clem Cheng, vice-president HR at Cigna Insurance, recounts a tale that shows how kindness and understanding can make a believer of any employee. 'I had just started in a new position with CIGNA some years ago. On my first day of work, I learned that my career-long mentor had died. Without any hesitation, my new manager sent me on a plane to attend the funeral. With the timing and travel involved my first week or work was basically lost. I knew immediately that I was working for the right manager.'

What does all this tell us?

Looking at what a cross-section of managers from all types of industries and experiences have said, it is pretty clear that there are consistent concerns about top management's approach. They seem to revolve around five key points:

- not keeping promises/saying one thing and doing another
- honest, open communication
- a lack of courage by top managers to tell it like it is
- not walking the talk
- rewarding/promoting the wrong people.

And those 'if I were CEO for the day' wishes, brought out three key points:

- TALK to the people
- LISTEN to the people
- Ask them 'what should I STOP doing?'

All of these are basic management responsibilities. If they are not being delivered on then there is something wrong with the people who are managing your business. As I have said earlier, I do think (and so do many others) that we are currently reaping the harvest of our inability to give those we erroneously call managers the right skills to manage people. This, on the evidence offered here, needs to be urgently addressed. What my research clearly shows is a major concern that basic management skills are missing from many so-

> *basic management skills are missing from many so-called managers. These people are doing daily damage to our organisational structures and they are demotivating our people*

called managers. These people are doing daily damage to our organisational structures and they are demotivating our people.

Both big business and SMEs suffer from this. The solution is to reintroduce people management skills into our organisations and reward people for their abilities in this area. Several companies – predominantly medium-sized – told me that they make overall employee satisfaction and individual team satisfaction components of the annual bonus of their managers. This is a trend that is set to increase.

Not keeping promises/saying one thing and doing another

I hear this from employees every single day of my life. It culminates in employee alienation, because they don't know what is going on, or what tomorrow will bring. It reminds me of the (true) employee assessment process where a manager writes of one of his subordinates, 'His people would follow him anywhere, but only out of curiosity to see what happens next!' The worst scenario is where this happens at the top of an organisation, so there is no clear vision, the horizon is hazy and no one is quite sure which direction the corporate ship is sailing in for very long.

However, it must be on the 'to do' list of every manager from the CEO down to make certain that employees know what is going on. Unless they do, you can never engage them.

Honest, open communication

I keep hearing the excuse, 'We can't tell everyone everything because it's confidential.' Rubbish! If you know then so do others. We work with bright, intelligent and curious people (we all say that's the type of employee we want) so don't be ambiguous. Tell the truth, even when it is bad news, because it all comes out sooner or later. You know it does, so why not get in with the first blow, before the rumours take over? But (as we will discuss in a more detail in Chapter 9) take care with your communications. Don't give it to some spotty kid or some external PR firm. Show you're serious and give it to a director or a vice-president.

Create a champion for open, honest communication and make them accountable for the truth. This is particularly important in SMEs where, often, there is no separate communications role. Make sure a partner or a board member takes an active responsibility for it.

A lack of courage by top managers to tell it like it is

Glossing over bad news, putting a spin on things, isn't good. My view is that plain, straight communication works every time. If your PR firm can't write plain English, fire them and get someone who can. If your internal communications people don't get the idea, fire them too. Personally, I get heartily sick and tired of gobbledegook PR speak. Who do they think they are talking to? Certainly not to the 'very best people', that you as an employer profess make up your workforce, or so you proclaim on your website. By the way when did you last go on your own website. Do it. You'll find it very revealing. I send employees on to their websites all the time, and they come back dazed and confused. 'This place is nothing like that,' is the usual feedback.

There is no doubt that some managers think that they still can – in the twenty-first century no less – pull the wool, or most probably its synthetic equivalent, over the eyes and ears of the employees. Please believe me – and go out and tell them – *it doesn't work!* Never has, never will. But people keep trying. Somehow, it would seem, we have decided in our little corporate corridors that dressing things up in a new way takes the sting out of unwelcome news. While there are many examples of corporations deliberately being, in their often peculiar way, economical with the truth, none beats this from the Dutch office furniture company Samas. Announcing the redundancy of 200 of its 3,800 staff, it didn't say it was firing them. In a burst of utter creative genius (albeit seriously misplaced) it was quoted as saying it was 'to lose 200 of its 3,800 staff through' (wait for it!) 'stimulated natural turnover.' Be honest, be open, say what you mean – you're firing them, but you're trying to dress it up and failing miserably.

Not walking the talk

This is possibly the big one. Managers who tell you to do something, watch you do it and then go off and do something else themselves. I see it everywhere. One of my good friends is the HR director for a large Swiss global business. Life was bad. There had been job cuts, cost cuts, you name it they had done it. As part of getting into the new spirit of austerity she gave back her car (and its attendant chauffeur). But most of the others did not. While cost cuts had got to the level of no free biscuits and coffee anymore, directors were still arriving at the front door of headquarters in their black, chauffeur-driven limos. There's a tram route right outside that building. Imagine how morale and productivity would have lifted if those directors had been seen alighting from a tram, having paid for their own coffee and newspaper on the way? Is that an extreme case? No, it happens every day. And often cuts are blindly made in a doomed attempt to show that everything is being taken very seriously indeed. At one firm I worked with, when the recession hit most of the managers were pretty good about cascading the bad news and answering employees' concerns. In fact they were so good that after the initial announcement, they managed to fire the entire internal communications staff! From being good at something they became non-communicative to a ludicrous degree. Only rapidly rising dissent amongst middle managers restored the internal communications function. They followed that up with the cancellation of the six-monthly get-togethers of senior management. A nice move you might think. Not so. Despite the firm's woes they were still recruiting to fill new business opportunities and the six-monthly meets were the most cost-effective way for new and old employees to meet and begin to get an understanding of the business.

The lesson to learn from all this is that, yes, you should walk the talk, do it like you expect others to do it. But don't go overboard and cut where it will do you damage. Another example is travel. When the going gets rough everyone flies economy. My view is that this is a crazy policy on long trips. You want people who will be ready to go and you want people who will be able to work while they are en route to a far off destination. I don't see automatic downgrades to economy class being a smart saving. I know engineers who regularly flew to places like China and India (up to twice a month in some cases) who, when the travel cheaper directive came in, first used their own air miles to secure upgrades. After that they quit.

Walking the talk sends the message that the leaders of a business are prepared to sacrifice too. It doesn't mean that you have to shut down everything or cannot make intelligent exceptions that help to get work done. We operate our businesses in complex, complicated and often-

Walking the talk sends the message that the leaders of a business are prepared to sacrifice too.

chaotic times, so we need flexibility in our decision-making. My suggestion is that you consider carefully what to cut and why. What is the longer-term impact on the business? What message does it send to different groups of people?

One final point on this subject: during research on a study[1] I made some interesting discoveries. Where people failed, or simply just chose not to walk the talk and join in with any plan, was in one of three distinct areas of any organisation:

- at the top of the organisation (hubris and arrogance of the 'I'm too important/senior for this stuff' variety)
- at the bottom of the organisation (nothing to lose, 'so what are they going to do, fire me?')
- with employees who have a great deal of contact externally, eg salespeople, on-site engineers, who know that they can virtually walk out at any time. Reason? They are always aware of new opportunities in rival firms and customer's operations. They are always the first to leave in any upturn.

Rewarding/promoting the wrong people

In 99 per cent of the business books I have read (and there have been a great many of them) there is one strange phenomenon at work: none of them mentions office politics. They espouse theories about how to manage. They even talk about clear goals and open and honest communication. But they don't talk about the politics of business. I can't imagine why. Because, like it or not, office politics are the very lifeblood of any organisation.

Personally, I have never seen a company that doesn't have office politics. It is a natural as breathing. Therefore, it is sad but true, people who don't deserve it will get promoted and rewarded. It is, as they say, in the nature of things. The boss likes Bill and he doesn't really like you. And even if you are the better man, you are not going to get that promotion. It is frustrating, but office politics won't go away just because we think it is a bad thing. All we can decently do is admit it exists and try to work towards a more honest solution, where the good guys do get the raise.

I am a frequent user of the train line from Bournemouth in southern England to London. One morning I was sitting in my compartment when two be-suited executives got in. Between 40 and 50, well dressed. They were also furious in a vicious kind of way. For over an hour they dished the dirt on every person they worked with – subordinates and superiors alike. No one was spared. These two executives were poorly led and felt that they had a right to do things their own way, rather than the way the company expected them to. I listened to them from behind my newspaper. And I got to thinking, 'These two people are surviving, yet they live for screwing up the lives of others. They are clearly out of control and they are in fact a major liability to their own firm (I never did find out who the firm was, much to my chagrin). What they needed was to be terminated. But who was going to do that? Was there anyone with the courage to stand up to them and say, 'Hey guys, it's all over?' Most probably not.

Then I recalled another conversation I had had some weeks earlier with a work colleague who said that the further you went up the organisation the safer – not the more vulnerable – you became. 'Senior executives don't get fired – it's too embarrassing. OK, you might put them somewhere safe where they can't do too much damage but they don't get fired.'

And you know, he was right. Senior people, unless they get caught with their hands in the cookie jar, don't get fired. They get cared for and looked after just like the two on the train.

So it isn't just a case of the wrong people getting rewarded or promoted. It is also a case of the wrong people being in the company at all. I guarantee you know only too well who they are in your business. So who has the courage to cut out the poison, or do you just put up with it as business as usual?

Being CEO for the day
TALK to the people

From the comments in the research, it is fairly obvious that many employees feel very removed from what senior management is up to. Since that series of interviews, more and more people have commented to me that there is not enough face-to-face communication between themselves and senior management, and this disconnect – whether real or just perceived – is a major concern. Certainly there are companies who do this very well, but in times of trouble there is a tendency for the CEO and his immediate cabal to circle the wagons on the top floor of headquarters and hunker down for the duration. In a modern-day organisation that is not a recipe for winning hearts and minds. Especially in parlous times senior management need to be out there doing that open, honest communication. It does pay off, if only in holding on to people when the good times come around again. Strange how many CEOs are just not very good at this sort of thing.

LISTEN to the people

What I found of more interest – but just as disturbing as the need for the CEO to talk – were the comments about listening. Again, I hear this all the time: 'Top management don't pay any attention, they never listen to our ideas or even when we voice concern about issues.' This is, frankly, pretty worrying. Employees on the ground, in touch with customers, suppliers and other stakeholders are the communication conduits of any business. Stop listening to them and you cannot know what is going on in your business world. No matter how well you manage the numbers, if you don't let your people reach you with news, ideas and just plain gossip and rumour you won't be able to take advantage of opportunities or steer around those great big rocks in the road. I constantly hear this complaint of management not listening and once more I think it is vital that senior management address the issue. All the smart managers I know meet with cross-sections of their employees once or twice a week. Of those that do, most say they get lots of good ideas and they also begin to find out what is really going on. Sitting up there in some ivory tower isn't going to glean you much information.

Ask them 'What should I STOP doing?'

When Clemens Reisbeck of Barclays Capital first suggested this one to me, I didn't really grasp the significance of it – I do now. In fact, this is a very powerful idea. 'What are the things I do, or members of my top management team do, that get in the way of you doing your job?' All of us should go around our companies and ask that question of a cross-section of 500 people. And if we don't think they'd tell us then we should make it an anonymous contribution process. I am certain than all of us get in the way at one time or another. But we are probably oblivious to the fact that our 'Well at headquarters it seemed like a great idea' decision, doesn't always play out in the divisions.

I think every business should launch a 'What should we stop doing?' campaign and see just what happens. For certain you will clear up a lot of problems and long-buried resentments.

What to do about this?

Hey, I'm not a management guru, I just report what I hear and try and make sense of it. Seems to me though that if we are getting these feelings from managers all over the place then there must be some substance to the notion that we have a long way to go in getting people's needs and expectations even half met. If I was a CEO – and I am not – I would spend some time thinking through what these views mean. Then I'd try and get them solved by committing top management to take real, positive action that is visible to the rank and file.

If you want to engage your employees, the only way you are going to do that is if they offer you at least some passing respect. But be honest with yourselves, tell yourself the truth, not the version you'd like to hear. If people are your key asset, for goodness sake take them, their views and who they are (those people who want to be themselves at work) seriously and then act on their contribution. Otherwise you are going to miss out and you won't have the right people to make your business a success.

Next we take a look at some of the ideas and concepts that seem to be able to play a part in hiring and holding people, with an emphasis on the need for flexibility in the workplace. Today's worker is very different from even 10 years ago; our policies and actions in the workplace need to reflect that.

> *If people are your key asset, for goodness sake take them, their views and who they are (those people who want to be themselves at work) seriously*

Good and bad management behaviour

Some of this – hopefully – will come as no surprise but research by UK-based management consulting firm Business Improvement Solutions (BIS) shows clearly that the most important thing good managers do well is COMMUNICATE. One of the things poor managers do badly is COMMUNICATE. Certainly in every employee survey over the years I have found that communication in one form or another tends to come at the top of the wish list.

However, BIS, in reporting their findings made a suggestion: why not 'reflect upon your own behaviour' as a supervisor or manager 'and consider which category you fall into.'

So here are BIS' good and bad manager behaviours. How do you think you would score with your people? Better still ask them to score you!

Behaviours that define the best managers

Open communicator	69%
Good team leader	55%
Positive personal qualities	55%[2]
Supportive	51%
Coach/mentor	43%
Even-handed	35%
Provide recognition	33%
Effective delegator	31%
Valued my opinions	29%
Provides feedback	29%
Objective focused	24%
Motivator	18%
Demonstrated trust	16%
Respect for work/life balance	16%

Behaviours that define the worst managers

Poor team leader	69%[3]
Poor personal qualities	69%[4]
Poor communicator	65%
Unsupportive	47%
Poor delegator	33%
Unbalanced feedback	33%
Lack of objectives or vision	31%
Not even-handed	29%
Poor coach/mentor	26%
Non-motivator	22%
No recognition	18%
Lack of trust	16%
Devalued my opinions	14%
Mean, not generous	14%

KEY ISSUES

- Management need to agree on and execute a compelling vision that employees can buy into.
- Five major gripes of management performance:
  - not sticking to promises
  - no communication
  - a lack of courage to take difficult decisions
  - not walking the talk (management hubris)
  - rewarding/promoting the wrong people.
- If CEO for the day employees would:
  - talk to people
  - listen to people
  - ask them, 'what should I STOP doing?
- Best managers are open communicators and good team leaders above all else.

Notes

1 (2001) *Social Capital: Securing Competitive Advantage in the New Economy.* Financial Times Executive Briefings.

2 All references in the Business Improvement Solutions study to managers being 'polite,' 'courteous', 'demonstrating honesty and integrity' are under this category.

3 Poor team leader includes phrases such as 'demoralising', 'uses team members as a scapegoat', 'treats staff like machines.'

4 Poor personal qualities includes phrases such as 'rude and self-centred', 'publicly berates staff', 'bullies people', 'untrustworthy' and 'lying.'

Chapter 4

It's their lifestyle **not** your workstyle that counts

To be what we are, and to become what we are capable of becoming, is the only end of life.

Robert Louis Stevenson

There is only one success, to be able to spend your life in your own way.

Christopher Morley

Where do we begin?

Having established that our employees are not necessarily going to swallow everything top management says and that they are going to be suspicious of many of our actions, where can we hope to begin in building a climate that thrives on engagement and commitment? The most obvious answer is for every organisation to realise that they are not managing in the same world as they were ten or even five years ago. Today's business climate is different. The people, the technology, the overall work environment have moved on. As I said in an earlier chapter, if there is one word that defines the next decade of work it is *flexibility*. And that flexibility comes into play in all sorts of ways:

- flexibility in lifestyle
- flexibility in time
- flexibility in work
- flexibility in reward.

But more than that, our employees now clearly define themselves by the lifestyles that they have chosen to lead. They no longer define themselves as engineers, chemists, pilots, nurses, teachers and the like. They define themselves through the lifestyle that meets their needs; the job they do, the career they opt for, is only a part of that. They are a gym-going, opera-loving, bicycle-riding, single mother of two, who also happens to be a biochemist; or a Harley-Davidson-riding, Herman Hesse-reading, 55-year-old grandfather, who also happens to be a vice-president of marketing for a supermarket chain. Their definition of who *they* are has changed forever. You can hire them and fire them, reward them and disappoint them, but they are still what they are. They are not yours. They don't say 'I'm a product manager with the XYZ corporation' anymore. That is *not* their identity, that's just how *you* define them, not how they define themselves. And in regarding them in this way you make a huge mistake. If you want to engage the new-age employee you will have to do better than that. If you want to gain their respect and consequently their commitment you have to know who they really are. Build from that premiss and you'll be a winner.

Our task as managers is to understand the needs and expectations of our employees, and would-be employees, and their chosen lifestyle. Set this understanding within the context of the subtle changes that have taken place in the last few years and we can then begin to create a work structure that allows for maximum flexibility. The task also involves a good dose of innovation and a willingness to adapt the way the employer approaches the job with the employee.

> Our task as managers is to understand the needs and expectations of our employees, and would-be employees, and their chosen lifestyle

Most of the available research I have consulted points to the SME category being more able to cope with these demands, because the smaller size of the firm frequently creates a family-type atmosphere. But this is not always the case. Often SMEs lack the financial and manpower resources to react quickly enough to emerging trends or to make effective decisions. The lifestyle revolution is no different. Far from identifying closely with your products or services some employees, at least, will find that the job is not what they get out of bed for five days a week. In an SME, this can have dramatic consequences.

Of course, there's been a focus on flexibility in business – both in the private and public sectors – before this. We've already seen trends like telecommuting, job-sharing, part-time work, interim and outsourced work, but this time it's different. Vast numbers of employees are redefining their lifestyles and consequently workstyles too. Whether this really is a post 9/11 and post economic recession reaction or just a huge new trend I am not sure. What I am sure about is that this is a major trend that will affect how, when and who we hire for our businesses in the future. Basically, it means that people everywhere will self-select employers on the basis of how they want to build their lives. Employers, therefore, who are not open to drastic change in how they run their businesses will see themselves starved of the very talent they require to succeed. Employers who make the changes in how they organise for work will earn the respect of their employees, they will become the new 'great places to work.' If we want to re-engage our workforces we have to be prepared to meet their needs more fully and far more flexibly than we do today.

However, not everyone wants to do that. According to Paul Smith, a director of recruiting firm Harvey Nash, some companies will go to all sorts of lengths to avoid flexible working. 'Employers have approached us' he told *The Guardian* newspaper, 'and asked if we can devise a way to skew the recruitment process in favour of young, single people, to keep parents and their demands for flexible working at bay. They also mention targeting gay people because they want to limit the risk of losing money through maternity and paternity leave and the extra costs of providing flexible working.'

Of course, this type of thing does go on. But you'll never make employer of choice using these kinds of tactics. It may work short term, but it won't help you create and nurture a committed, engaged workforce.

But dinosaur companies aside, if there are any doubts about the necessity of a new approach a 2003 study by Towers Perrin[1] of 35,000 workers described levels of engagement in this way: 'A key focus of [the] research was measuring the respondents' level of engagement in their work. Just under a fifth of our total respondent group – a disturbingly small percentage – are highly engaged, freely giving that extra effort on an ongoing basis. An equal number are disengaged, meaning they have probably checked out from their work, as so many employers fear. The remainder – roughly two-thirds – are "moderately" engaged at best.'

The Towers Perrin study goes on to ask the ultimate question: why does engagement matter so much? 'Because', they conclude, 'engagement remains the ultimate prize for employers. Companies may use different names or define it slightly differently, but the endgame is the same for everyone – discretionary effort.' Then they add, 'But employees' willingness to deliver is neither infinite nor self-renewing. And the flip side of the coin – diminishing co-operativeness and engagement – is all about risk for the employer. Risk that the moderately engaged will slide toward increasing disengagement. Risk that resiliency will harden into recalcitrance. Risk that job performance will erode over time. Risk that as the economy rebounds, less than fully engaged employees will seek other employment.'

Finally, Towers Perrin conclude that 'the challenge lies with the large number of moderately engaged [whom they term the "massive middle"]. Left to their own devices,' they suggest, 'these employees could easily slide toward the wrong end of the engagement scale. Indeed, the sheer size of this group – probably the single largest group in any organisation – means it will have a disproportionate impact on the mood and morale of the workforce overall. Strengthening this group's level of engagement may be the most critical task virtually every employer faces today.'

My view is that much of this engagement, much of this commitment, will be generated from being open to new ways to meet – within your workplace – the lifestyle choices of your employees. Accommodate their lifestyle into your workstyle and you will begin to earn not just engagement, but respect, as an employer who cares about the one thing that's most important to them – their lives.

Without our very best efforts as employers (aided, no doubt by ever cheaper technology) to meet the expectations of the individuals we employ on a case-by-case basis (that will change and metamorphose at different times in their lives) we will never be able to recruit and retain effectively. And we are not talking here about allowing the odd extra day off or extra vacation time. Changing demographics and fast-moving social trends mean that we have to have plans that meet these new developments head on. An ageing European population means that we will have to work longer (so we will need to know how to employ the over-60s). Changing legislation on gay marriages complicates benefit programmes. An increasing number of divorces, re-marriages, single mothers and sandwiched employees (faced with child and elder care simultaneously), mean that those we seek to employ are part of whole new niches in society. We no longer employ thousands of John

We no longer employ thousands of John and Jean Smith look-a-likes. We employ a diverse mix of individuals

and Jean Smith look-a-likes. We employ a diverse mix of individuals, all with different needs. Let's look at these emerging issues of work, reward, time and lifestyle and develop some understanding of what lies ahead.

Flexibility in work, time and lifestyle

In many ways, flexibility in work, time and lifestyle all fit together, because today most employees see work as an extension of who they are. People go for jobs that meet their criteria and, as they have considerably more choice these days, the job defines their attitudes and personality. Want hip? You go to a high technology start-up or a new media operation. Want sensitive? A healthcare firm or a not-for-profit organisation. Just want lots of money? An investment bank. As Jonas Ridderstrale and Kjell Nordstrom explain in their best-selling book *Funky Business*[2] 'people want to be themselves at work.' They are no longer defined by the job they do, they are defined by who they are. This is why employee branding is such hard work. Just as it was invented, the employee said, 'Hey, I'm not a McDonalds or an IBM or a British Airways brand carrying employee, I'm me. And that is who I am going to be from now on.' They don't necessarily want their hearts and minds won. They want to contribute, but they don't always want to be a part of your club, just because you think they should. Managers of SMEs need to heed this. There is an almost unhealthy belief that employees of SMEs like the cosy closeness of this type of business. Well they might have done once, but this MTV watching, mouse-clutching generation is after a lot more than a cosy feeling. Sure, you might provide the financial incentive, but they want more than that; a lot more, and they are out to get it. So you are vulnerable unless you begin to tweak the 'we're all in this together' model. You might be in it, but your employees are very likely looking at a different set of criteria for fulfilling their expectations.

So these people – whom you are actively seeking to engage in wealth creation for your shareholders – have very distinct views of what work is all about. Sure they will do it, lots of it. But it is going to have to be on their terms, not yours. While in recessions management can get away with just about anything, come economic upturns and labour shortages the boot moves quickly to the other foot.

Work/life balance, NO; life/work balance YES

There has been a great deal written and spoken about work/life balance in recent years. It was taking off in a big way as a trend just prior to this last recession. Parlous times buried it before it really kicked in. Good thing too, it was the wrong way around! By that I mean that to our employees (these people we say we want to engage and earn respect from) the 'life' bit comes first and the 'work' thing second. The reason we got it the wrong way around was that it was written from the corporate, not the individual's, perspective. It is imperative to realise that, if we are going to make this engagement thing successful, it begins with the employees' lifestyles, and what they consider worth investing in. Stressing work as the starting point doesn't begin to get close to any kind of balance as far as individuals are concerned. Trying to sell a concept of work/life balance only disconnects the employee, imposing a concept that is not his or her reality or view of life.

Sensible managers I have discussed the work/life balance view with don't agree with it anyway. Most believe, and have told me, that if you hire smart people they will find, define and execute their own work/life balance equation whatever a company may feel to the contrary. My view is that the equation begins with each individual's lifestyle and that this governs all the workstyle issues. So, if there is any balance it is lifestyle/workstyle. If we make this the starting point we might just have some chance of engaging people who have an increasingly independent approach to life and work. True, there may be times in a person's life when the balance isn't there. Due to circumstances they are overworked and stressed. But rarely do these periods last for long. Today's employee knows how to make the choices that get their chosen lifestyle/workstyle back on track.

Within this context, flexibility at work means just that. Eight to four, nine to five doesn't work anymore. Well not all the time, at least. Virtually everyone I know has some kind of flexible schedule, to meet their lifestyle/workstyle needs. And it might not even be the lifestyle/workstyle they have chosen, but one forced on them by external circumstances. The big one is childcare. The arrival of a bouncing baby has the equivalent impact of an H-bomb on the average family. But if the employer values the employee, they can resolve the situation. Similarly, elder care (especially with people living longer) is becoming a major issue. Again, with goodwill on both sides this can

We have talked for years about empowering the employee. Guess what? They have empowered themselves. They are empowered and they have done it all on their own.

be worked out. With available technology employees in even the most sensitive jobs can work from home or another remote location. The alternative is they quit and go work for someone who can provide the flexibility they need.

We have talked for years about empowering the employee. Guess what? They have empowered themselves. They *are* empowered and they have done it all on their own.

The commuting issue is a similar one. Main business centres (Amsterdam, Brussels, Paris, London, Frankfurt, New York, Zurich and so on) are practically at gridlock status. Any sane employer who wants productive employees must see that one, two or three working days spent at home is a very wise alternative. Again, as employees formulate what **they** want, not what **you** want, they will make choices based on their own real-life ambitions. Whether that includes a future with your firm depends very much on your attitude. Your attitude to them fulfilling their lifestyle/workstyle scenario, which, remember, is unique to each person.

But one word of advice. Please, please, please make sure that in defining flexible work practices that you have a policy. Don't do ad hoc deals with employees. These breed resentment and accusations of favouritism. I have even seen protests in offices from single women saying that those that have children get better treatment 'because they are allowed to work from home if the child is sick.' So make it a formal option, then everyone knows what the rules are. And remember there will always be those who want to be 'in an office', if only for the social cohesion it brings to their lives. Which of course is yet another individual's lifestyle choice. Some years ago I wrote a book about telecommuting[3] and made the huge error in an early version of suggesting that remote working would be terrific for handicapped people, particularly those confined to wheelchairs, as it would allow them to do a normal day's work from home. Furious wheelchair users complained bitterly. The last thing – it emerged – they wanted to do was be stuck at home. They wanted to be in an office with other people for the buzz of social contact!

It's all about convenience

And here is the key to the whole 'where-I-work' issue: it isn't static, it will change depending on the individual's current requirements. In a previous book *Talent Magnet*[4] I pointed out that changing circumstances in an individual's life can seriously affect whether or not they choose to work with you. In that book, I referred to the fact that a single person, living in a city, would be happy to go to work each day in that city. But as lives change, so do expectations. I described one such situation where the single person marries and immediately needs to find a bigger place, which possibly means a longer commute. Later the couple decide to have children, which probably means a move to the suburbs. All this defines whether or not the person now wants to make that commute or find another work option to meet their emerging lifestyle needs.

Interestingly enough, not long after I wrote that, one of my publishers decided to quit its central London offices and head for a brand new headquarters in a system-built industrial park 50 or more miles out of the city. Most of its staff were single, and few had children. Average age was probably 28–30. What no one in management took into account was that these people would (a) have to reverse commute out of London and (b) would not be in a place where they could meet their friends after work or at lunchtime. The new location – looking good on paper by surrendering expensive London real estate – was entirely what the employees didn't want from their lifestyle. Result? Even though media jobs were scarce at the time, over 70 per cent of the employees took the redundancy package that the company legally had to offer (because the move was over a certain distance). It is probably the best illustration I have seen of an organisation not realising that the numbers don't matter – the people do. If you can't satisfy employee expectations you won't be able to engage them and seek their commitment to the job. In fact you will actively destroy your key asset– your people. Why? Because you made it inconvenient to get to work and ruined their lifestyle/workstyle needs and expectations.

One further point. Several people have asked me if allowing people to work in different, more flexible, ways and places means that a working relationship deteriorates over time. My view is that a lot depends on how you set it up. Set policy and procedure on this and get a real contract. But also don't forget that in this lifestyle/workstyle world relationships will change anyway, as the person's needs and expectations shift. No one today lives in a static situation for very long, so people's lifestyle expectations are in a constant state of flux. Whether, as an employer, you choose to meet those expectations as they change is up to you.

Time gentlemen, please

Time. In this fast-paced world we never seem to have enough of it. So it has become a very valuable commodity. So valuable that more and more people are realising that it is too valuable to spend working. Now if you are thinking, 'But I read all the time that people are working longer, and longer hours,' you'd be right. What I am saying – and what people tell me – is they may be working long hours, but they have no plans for this state of affairs to last forever. Most people, most employees, deep down inside, have a plan. And it doesn't necessarily include a career in your business.

Already in countries like Belgium and The Netherlands three- and four-day working weeks are government approved for those that want them (for those over 40 at any rate), which means that there has been a huge rise in job sharing. Part of the reason for this is something that bosses often don't understand: the lack of ambition in much of our society.

Basically, many of your employees are very happy if they can contribute, but they don't want their hearts or minds won, they just want to do the job, get paid, go fishing and take their vacations (two or three times a year) on some sun-kissed beach. As they reach a certain age, most of the important and expensive purchases of life are taken care of (in addition their spouse probably works too). So they don't need the money, or not as much as they used to. So what do you do? You ask to work three or four days a week and you use the rest of the time to go fishing, or whatever.

There is increasing evidence that this is the way people are going to choose to work. So if you as an employer aren't ready, these people will find a way to meet their own expectations without you.

A survey in the UK by the Department of Trade and Industry in 2004 found that 70 per cent of workers would like more time off to pursue an arts hobby, and 38 per cent have already changed their working hours to accommodate outside interests. If any other proof were required a Graduate Career survey in 2003 discovered that graduates value work flexibility over pay and that the British (who allegedly have the longest working week in Europe) would rather work more sensible hours than win the nation's lottery.

It seems pretty clear that employers who fail to heed this groundswell of need are going to find it tough when competing for people.

And Britain isn't alone in thinking working hours don't work out. Europeans think so too. Students polled in Belgium, France and Germany by their student unions said they would prefer to work a four-day week, if that was possible. Maybe political apathy has spread to work as well?

There is also a trend for people to request longer vacation periods, or to go on sabbaticals. Equally, the idea of leaving a company for six or nine months and then hoping to pick your job up when you return is gaining popularity. 'She's gone travelling for six months,' when you call someone's office is an answer I am now hearing all the time.

And this has been followed by a steep rise in interim assignments. René Grootaert, managing director of Ernst & Young Executive Temporary Management observes that interim management is now in its second generation and it has changed. 'Up to five years ago temporary executives were exclusively from the ranks of people who had been made redundant by their companies,' he explained. 'Today there are young people going straight from university. They like the flexibility. Some of them work an assignment for six to nine months and then take three to six months off. For them it is a lifestyle thing and they have no plans to change that.'

This type of flexibility makes a great deal of sense to employers though. When skills are needed for a new assignment or project, you can quickly hire a contract manager who can do the job and doesn't expect to be around in a year's time. If employees can be flexible like this employers can gain as well.

Just give me the time and keep the money

Another phenomenon that is emerging – especially in European countries where personal taxation is high – is the trend to exchange salary for time. 10 per cent of salary in exchange for a specific number of days' vacation. Sheila Bates, an HR professional, who developed this concept for the mobile phone provider KPMOrange in the Benelux comments

'We employed a lot of young, single people and the one commodity in short supply is time. In a high-taxed country like Belgium giving up a slice of your cash income isn't that hard, because it is getting whacked for tax anyway.' She continues, 'Younger employees always have a shortage of time to get things done, and this we found was a great motivator and a great way to retain people by giving them what they wanted – meeting their needs in a flexible, yet structured fashion.'

What all these developments show is that we must to be able to react to and meet these changing employee wish lists as and when they arise. The respect we need to garner from our new-age employees is partly going to arise from being seen to go the extra mile in order to meet their expectations.

It's an age thing too

If flexibility in work, time and lifestyle all fit together, they get blown apart quickly when it comes to one thing – AGE. Remember the good old, bad old days when you joined a company and the kind lady from the personal department gave you a little booklet and said, 'Now these are the company guidelines. Read them and if you have any questions let me know.' That was it. Everyone was treated more or less the same way. Well you can't do that anymore.

In recognition of that, some years ago I developed a list of categories of people. While admitting that some of us slop over the edges of these groupings somewhat, depending on circumstances, they still seem to reflect the different age groups we employ:

- twinkies   under 20
- point'n'clickers   20–25
- generation X   25–35
- middle-aged and manic 35–45
- growing old frantically   45–55
- grey tops   over 55.

What these categories have in common is that they each need a tailored approach, because they all have different needs. If we want to engage them and seek out their commitment we need plans to help them achieve their current goals.

Twinkies (under 20s, also known as cyber-kids)

These people have grown up with a mouse welded to the palm of their right hand. They don't play by our rules, but they are the generation after next of the managers and specialists in our workforce. How do we appeal to this type of person?; how do we deal with face-to-face interaction with them, never mind employing them? We are going to have to learn, because we won't have any option. Now, look at it this way. If you don't understand your kids, then you are in trouble, but here's the lifeline. Beloit College in Wisconsin has for many years done a great public service. Every year, they publish the Mindset List to its faculty and staff as an indicator of the many ways in which entering 17- and 18-year-olds see the world differently from their professors, coaches and mentors. The list is a reminder that the worldview held by today's new college students is significantly different from the intellectual framework of those students who entered only a few years earlier. This will help you understand where you need to begin and why the disconnect between management's views and that of the employees is so radical. On the other hand it might just frighten you off!

For someone born in 1984, consider these facts.

- Richard Burton, Ricky Nelson and Truman Capote have always been dead.
- Cars have always had eye-level rear stoplights, CD players, and air bags.
- The 'evil empire' has moved from Moscow to a setting in some distant galaxy.
- 'Big Brother' is merely a television show.
- Cyberspace has always existed.
- Barbie has always had a job.
- George Foreman has always been a barbecue grill salesman
- There has always been an heir to the heir to the British throne.
- China has always been a market-based reforming regime.
- Nicolas Cage, Daryll Hannah, Eddie Murphy, and John Malkovich made their first major films the year you were born.
- The 'Fab Four' are not a male rock group from Liverpool, but four women enjoying 'Sex and the City'.
- A 'hotline' is a consumer service rather than a phone used to avoid accidental nuclear war.
- The drug 'ecstasy' has always been around.

- Genetic testing and DNA screening have always been available.
- Magnetic Resonance Imaging (MRI) has always been available to doctors.

So, how challenging do you think employing today's Twinkies is going to be? But let's remember we must not look at it like that. What Mr or Ms Employer need to work out is what do you have to do to meet these people's expectations; can you fit your work requirements into their lifestyles? Now there's a great project for some smart, newly minted MBA, wouldn't you say? Of course this is a pretty Anglo-centric list, but wherever you are try and match it. Then you'll get some idea of the task ahead if you are to engage these people.

Point'n'clickers (20–25)

This category has already invaded our workspace. And to meet their requirements we have to be very, very flexible. Many of the best and brightest will quite happily quit a job and go hiking for 12 months just for the hell of it. The way to reach them is to understand them and make it easy for them to do their job. Also realise that, more than ever, this 20–25-and-over age-group (at least the bright ones that we want) are migrating to major centres of population. I'll talk more about the 'importance of place' later, but there are key locations emerging where the younger talent wants to hang out with each other. London, New York, LA, Brussels, Zurich, Milan and Barcelona all fall into this 'magnet' category. This age group is not daunted by travel or crossing borders, in fact to them it is normal (they'll happily go from London to Paris to a club for a Saturday night). Countries don't really exist for them, national borders don't have any real resonance (especially true in an ever-enlarging European Union).

In fact, if you can engage them. by being ultra-flexible in the way you employ them, they will reward you in return. They are immensely flexible themselves in their outlook, unfazed by new experience and very often multi-lingual and with a love of challenge. What you will find is that whether they began life in Moscow or Madrid, Lubliana or London, the best and brightest think and talk in the same way, and share the same expectations.

My view is that you badly need these people – far more badly than they need you – in your business. How you find and keep them is up to you. Personally, I'd start by making someone responsible for locating them, establishing the kind of offers you would want to put on the table and researching – for your industry – the kind of work conditions you would need to maintain.

Generation X (25–35)

Was Generation X a myth? With the benefit of hindsight it probably was. It was youth getting the social sciences workover. However, whatever you want to call it, 'it' is getting older. Now in the 25–35 tunnel it is beginning to take on new responsibilities, and it is possibly carrying the usual social and financial baggage of partner, children, home, mortgage and school fees. But it still holds different views from its elders. While happy to put in an honest day's work for an honest day's pay, it exacts a price. It takes vacations, long-weekends and usually has an all-consuming out-of-work interest. As I explained earlier, life to the Generation X-er comes before work. Most likely, this is the employee category that will force us to make the most changes. They *will* want to work at home (as both partners will normally have careers) and they will want to be able to dovetail their work and leisure patterns. But we as employers will be able to meet those needs (technically we already can, it is perhaps just the company culture that might need a makeover), and in return there is no reason why we won't be respected and appreciated for that. The way to deal most easily with this group is to consult them. Notoriously, employee surveys tend to ask people *en masse* what they want and then try and break it down by different groups. A different approach is required here: a series of face-to-face discussions to establish 'needs and wishes'. If you don't know what they are you can't resolve any resentments, bad feelings or pent-up desires. Better to air these things, even if you can't deliver everything that people would like.

Middle-aged and manic (35–45)

When I first used this phrase people objected. They don't now. They've become part of the category themselves and understand. The age 35–45 can be extremely stressful in good times or bad. Basically this is because it is your last chance to clamber up the ladder, if that is your goal, or to establish yourself in your professional field. At the same time your lifestyle is likely to lurch around quite a lot as you probably set up house (we can't just say 'married' any more) with a partner, probably have children and worry about your rapidly ageing parent(s). In many ways this group is fairly acquiescent (I would hesitate to use the word grateful), because if it is in safe and secure employment there is one less thing for it to worry about. So the trick to meeting the needs of this group and creating the right cultural climate for them is to reassure and make them feel safe and needed. That phrase about 'celebrating small victories and milestones' has never been truer. A cynical person might suggest that making a fuss over them and conscientiously acknowledging achievements is probably the best way to ensure their commitment to the business.

Growing old frantically (45–55)

Here we are with the survivors of various battles and downturns. These people know their stuff and in many cases are virtually fireproof. If they are smart, they have a little tucked away, they are probably still on the original pension plan (before it got diluted these last years for newcomers). Their children are possibly through college, their mortgage is dwindling and if both partners work they are safe (as if one gets fired they'll collect a nice 'goodbye' package). That's why getting these people to change is so tough. They don't like surprises, but they will respond to being dealt with fairly. It is for this category that the honest and open communication and unambiguous decision-making that I wrote about in Chapter 3 becomes most critical.

The other thing that must not be forgotten about this group is that they are the corporate conscience and its history rolled into one. Want to know where things are, who knows the answer? This group will tell you. However, these people know their value and they may just be tempted to leave you for 'one last fling' with a competitor if the right offer comes along. To that end they are vulnerable. Therefore, again you need to know about their plans. Would they – for example – appreciate going onto a four-day week, where they could use their skills but get in a little more leisure time? Would it be a good idea to find out before they ask you? My view is, be proactive. Don't wait. This indicates that you as a business care about them as an individual. If it isn't a three- or four-day week, what would make them more committed to the firm? Do they want to work toward an early retirement or a part-time job; would they really like to relocate (and could you help them continue to make a contribution to the firm from that new location)? If you don't know what the need is you will never be able to meet it (rarely are they revealed until they are well on the way to being realised).

Grey tops (55 and over)

There are so many over 55s out in the workplace these days that I think I need to realign my categories somewhat. Many of them didn't plan to be here at all, but pension crises and a falling stock market have meant that many have had no choice but to stay in work. But, for those that want to, there is nothing wrong with that. They are fitter than any previous generation and could happily go on until 70-plus if their health holds out. However, my view is that our firms need to find roles for these people that celebrate their knowledge and enthusiasm, but also ensure that they don't clog up the succession process and prevent the younger generation having a go. In that way, I think that all businesses, intent on keeping older managers, need to put them into almost ambassadorial roles, where they can mentor and act as internal consultants, all the while letting those below manage the business. And this again can be achieved by discussion and consultation, teasing out what is best for them and best for the business. I know two very active 60-year-olds who run the coaching programme for their firms, usually only appearing physically one or two days a week. I know a German, now retired, in California who is the 'internal guru' for his organisation's management development process. Elsewhere, companies have found what amount to second careers for ageing executives, where they can use their knowledge and their contacts to help close deals and innovate new products. I think that as long as they have clear roles and responsibilities, they can be fully engaged and committed – and everyone wins. But success with this group does require a formal plan.

Keep abreast of employee lifestyle expectations

In all this it would seem that current six-monthly or annual reviews are not adequate, in most cases, for establishing enough about future wants and needs. Most performance reviews concentrate on tasks and results. They are very specific. In other areas they assess people management abilities. What is most probably needed is not another review but an opportunity at least once each year to ask some open-

If we can track an employee's changing expectations we can truly engage with them. Hey! We might even make them respect us again!

ended questions about an employee's world. Because if lifestyle comes ahead of workstyle then we need to know what the big issues are, the emerging issues, the 'life' issues of that person. If we can track an employee's changing expectations we can truly engage with them. Hey! We might even make them respect us again!

It's the geography, stupid!

Earlier I referred to the disaster that one firm visited upon itself by not taking into account employees' expectations and forcing them to make the choice of changing lifestyle or leaving (they chose the latter). This emphasises the fact that location plays a huge role in a company's ability to acquire true commitment. That particular firm actually moved to really great offices. The fact that you could see cows grazing from the windows rather than the line of trendy restaurants they had left behind in Covent Garden simply underlined that, not only had they lost the plot, they never had one to begin with. In the last few weeks I have witnessed two new recruits at a major headquarters quit after week one because they were taking up to an hour to leave the firm's car park at rush hour. This was something they were not prepared to put up with and they moved on. Certainly the sheer drudgery of commuting into most major cities (not to mention the cost) means that if other opportunities arise, employees are more likely to take the plunge and leave. Once again it depends on what sort of employees you want and what their expectations are.

Single people have no real desire (well not many anyway) to live and work in the middle of nowhere. It just isn't practical for the lifestyle they have chosen to lead. They naturally congregate where there are more people like themselves. This doesn't mean that single people only want to live and work in major cities where worklife and nightlife are great. You will have seen for yourself that there are thousands of single young people filling jobs in resorts from Fort Lauderdale to Faro. But again this is the lifestyle option they have chosen for a certain, probably limited, period of time. Some of them may possibly stay forever, others will move on. But their experiences and new, emerging, expectations will mean that they will rarely return to their roots. So as employers, we have to be clear about the type of people we want and we have to be sure that our location ensures a ready supply of that type of person. Then we have to be confident that we can create an employment offer that is attractive and lasting.

When times are harsh people will take anything they can. When times are good, the choices multiply. If we are to engage and excite people we must have a really good proposition and be prepared to adapt it quickly and radically if necessary.

Banking on a smooth transition

Even when you create the perfect office environment for those you seek to attract and retain, you have to maintain that position because there will always be someone doing it better. A good case in point is bankers Lehman Brothers. They moved into their new London headquarters at Canary Wharf from their old building in Liverpool Street in the City in late 2003. Not one employee failed to make the transition. The reason was that the firm had spent a great deal of time planning the move and making sure that it took people's needs (including their lifestyle needs) into account. It also meant changing for good some of the old habits. 'We used to have a ritual of the Monday morning meeting,' said managing director and head of HR for Europe, Tony Fogel. He continued, 'Now we still have the meeting, but you don't have to be there, you can just dial in and take part on-line.' More than that, the travel time is little affected for most employees and there are adequate car park facilities. Also Lehman Brothers have already invested heavily in secure technology so employees can work from home, and that includes full-time working mothers who spend all or part of their time working from home. Other innovations and practical ideas that have kept turnover at the firm low are an emergency childcare unit (which Lehman shares with two other firms), so if a nanny goes sick or there is another personal crisis, full-time help is available. Additionally, employees can sign on with the company-appointed doctor who works on site and there is another for alternative homeopathic medicine as well. The company also has the, by now virtually obligatory, employee gym and in-house noodle and sushi bars. External to the Lehman Brothers' tower the entire shopping mall complex and transportation links of Canary Wharf are accessible without going outside into the open air – a boon in bad weather.

Essentially the success of Lehman Brothers' transition has been based entirely on knowing the lifestyle choices that their people have made and tailoring the employee proposition to make it work. It is a perfect example of how to become, and remain, a magnet for talent.

Barbecues by the lake

In other, less crowded, environments it can be easier to employ in one place a cross-section of people with different lifestyle needs. In Zurich, where many banks and insurance companies are clustered around the lake, employees (mainly the younger ones) go swimming in the lake at lunchtime. Not only that, many of the firms operate barbecues in the car parks in the summer. In a city where the local free paper is called '20', because that is the average commute time, people work in a more stress-free environment, because that is what they have chosen to do. It meets their lifestyle requirements. It would take a lot to prise these people away from that lifestyle/workstyle equation to a noisy financial centre like London or New York.

It's a family lifestyle thing too

Still in Switzerland, pharmaceutical giant Novartis is the dominant employer in the small city of Basel. Veronica Foote, their British-born head of global staffing says that, 'It can be difficult for transfers and new recruits to get used to Basel and the area, but if they stay for six months they are hooked – especially employees with families.' Why? Novartis have gone out of their way to meet employees' lifestyle expectations (especially those they seek to recruit from outside Switzerland). 'We have a very good English/German school,' says Foote, 'and housing is relatively inexpensive compared to London or New York.' Novartis has also put an emphasis on families, bringing the whole family to Basel to see and sample the school and local facilities. 'Families make decisions today as a collective group, so we spend time with them,' she enthuses. 'What we are trying to do is to tailor-make our recruitment strategy on the basis of what people are looking for as a lifestyle, not what we, Novartis, wants. Also it is a very secure, safe environment with wonderful countryside.' This meets fully the criteria of the people they need to recruit. They have made the proposition fit the lifestyle expectations of the employees. 'We even have a fully staffed service to help the spouse find work, one way or another,' she adds, 'In this we share a job opportunity bank with other local employers.'

Easing the commute

At Bristol-Myers Squibb they also involve the employees' children in the 'buy' decision. 'We ask them to come and visit the area, because they are influencers in the decision too,' says Sunita Malhotra, director of HR at the firm's headquarters 10 miles south of Brussels. She explains, 'When we moved from eight locations to one, completely new, location, we asked every employee about where they lived, the length of their commute, the transport they used and how accessible the new site would be.' She went on, 'We had no relocation issues because we did good research and got any potential problems solved before we relocated.' Again, Bristol-Myers Squibb got involved in finding out the needs of their people and making that a part of their employment offer.

In other firms, getting employees deeply involved in fitting out the offices, or being given small budgets to 'personalise' their workspace adds to the overall feeling of 'they want me to be here.' An employee is far more likely to be committed to the job if they can bring even a small slice of their own lifestyle to work every day.

Into that debate come new ideas of what the ideal 'office' should be. Many experts – architects and office space planners – say that for today's employee the less celebration of hierarchy the better. They believe that executive floors, corner offices and executive dining rooms function symbolically to heighten the separation between top management and 'the rest'. An office that is built to separate, flatly contradicts stated corporate beliefs of openness and the breaking down of staffing levels. But today's employees see their lifestyle set in a classless meritocracy. Send other signals from your penthouse eerie at your peril.

A recent study by British Telecom found that workers on different floors of the same building had only a 1 per cent chance of meeting each other on any given day. If you are trying to get employees to interact, building physical and class barriers is not the way to do it.

And size of firm doesn't matter at all. Whether you have 50, 500 or 5,000 employees, meeting their needs is paramount. The compensation is that your efforts will be rewarded.

Too flexible? Yes, so stop it!

Of course in office space flexibility, as in other areas of employee engagement, things can, and do, go wrong. The senior management at advertising agency Chiat/Day mandated 'hot desking' for its employees, thinking that making any desk available to anyone on a first-come, first-served basis would generate a climate of creative energy. Employees hated the plan from day one, particularly as groups who needed to work together couldn't achieve what they wanted from randomly chosen desks. So members of teams came to the office early to claim desks that couldn't be reserved. When new managers took over, they quickly scrapped the practice.

Another foolish example was the check-in staff wildcat strike at British Airways: a great example of how to turn a happy, friendly group of workers into resentful militants overnight. British Airways wanted to introduce a computerised staffing system. What existed was a bizarre, yet efficient, system run by the staff themselves. Not well paid, but loyal, the staff had created an arbitrage system where if they needed extra time off or to move a schedule they would call each other until they found someone to take over their shift. The system worked, but British airways felt that it had lost control of the workforce. Poor communication and lack of understanding as to what this group of employees would lose in work flexibility led to deadlock and employees going on a wildcat strike. 'These people worked in relatively poorly paid jobs because they had one great advantage – flexibility,' said a manager who witnessed the strike.' British Airways removed that flexibility, with their plan, and that triggered the strike.'

As British Airways quickly discovered, flexibility is valued highly in our life/work world. Take it away, and you've got trouble.

Wellness is goodness

More than that, smart employers are emulating their employees' lifestyle choices in other ways too. The healthy, keep-fit lifestyle of many employees has prompted switched-on employers to adopt it within the business as well. For example, wellness programmes, where corporations actively seek to promote both mind and body health, are increasing dramatically. Says Anthony Phillips, managing director of WellKom Corporate Services, 'managers are realising that they need to be proactive in developing personal wellness management capabilities in their firms. We work on the basis that well people are more likely to be productive and committed to a business.'

Many of these are clearly an extension of what employees have created for themselves as part of their own lifestyle choices. Now some pioneering, innovative companies see that extending this to the workplace makes a much more all-inclusive proposition to the employee. What the employer is saying is, 'please bring your own, personal lifestyle with you when you come to work and we will support that in the best ways we can.'

Having said that, there is still a long, long way to go for the average company to promote any kind of wellness inside their four walls. A January 2004 survey carried out by the web portal HR Gateway[5] reported that three-quarters of respondents said their organisation did not incentivise staff with free/discounted gym membership off-site as part of a benefits package. The same percentage was true for in-house fitness centres. Lower-level employees were not the only ones to suffer. Over two-thirds of senior managers didn't receive these types of incentives either. Worse still, the survey noted that, 'although usually tasked with spreading a culture of work-life balance and well-being around an organisation, HR is a long way from practising what it preaches, with only 15 per cent taking a full lunch break every day.'

Making the reward structure flexible

The first thing to realise when talking about reward is that we are not just referring to monetary compensation. Both

> *The first thing to realise when talking about reward is that we are not just referring to monetary compensation.*

employers and employees today see reward as much more than plain old-fashioned cash in the bank. But again, we also have to stress that it is those who can be most flexible and treat employees as individual cases requiring tailored compensation in different ways and at different times in their lives that will truly create the engagement culture we would all like.

As with the changing needs of an employee's overall lifestyle and its relationship to workstyle, so compensation will need to be restructured on a regular basis to reflect emerging needs. Compensation consultants Towers Perrin explain that 'over the past decade, more and more companies have begun viewing their reward programmes as an aggregated investment pool that they can mix and remix in different ways, depending on the workforce needs and issues and financial pressures. They can identify employee preferences among reward options and create programmes that let employees trade current for deferred pay, salary for bonuses, bonuses for benefits, benefits for cash and so on.' Towers Perrin add, 'Down the road lies perhaps the ultimate goal. A totally customised, flexible approach that puts all the risk and responsibility in employees' hands by giving them a total sum of money – commensurate with their skills, experience, function and level – to allocate in whatever way best suits their needs across an array of employer-provided, or sponsored, programmes.'

By being a great deal more flexible in how and when they reward people at different stages in their life, companies will be able better to meet employee needs, once again allowing the employee to fulfil the lifestyle option they have chosen at that particular time. For example, a young, single professional may want more cash incentives as well as increased blocks of time off (back to trading salary for time). When that professional settles down with a partner, they may want a cheap loan for a house, or some guarantee to cover school fees for children. Later pension or other after-work provisions may well take precedence. As people's needs change and their lifestyle options develop as they move through life, so companies can change the mix.

Of course, not everyone has signed up to the concept of flexible reward. A study by Aon Consulting[6] highlighted what they called, 'the sorry state of compensation planning.' According to their study, 40 per cent of businesses developed their compensation policies more than five years ago, and almost 50 per cent more than four years ago. Worse still, although aligning compensation programmes with corporate goals frequently shows up on HR and Finance's 'wish-lists,' 61 per cent of the respondents felt that gaps still existed: 40 per cent to a great extent. Aon commented, 'these numbers suggest the need for a fresh and focused look at compensation planning.'

Not just money

Cash may be king, but it isn't the only reward item in today's world. Other factors – the flexible approach to time, the where and when employees do the job – form part, in their minds at least, of the reward structure. Certainly, in making job choices, employees today compare offers based not just on the monetary input but the convenience of working for a particular employer. Furthermore, access to the very best training and development (of which more in Chapter 5), is regarded as reward by many. So too is coaching or access to a mentoring programme. All of these 'add-ons' have a strong intrinsic value, but again their value varies depending on the expectations of the individual involved. However, there is no doubt that companies who place strong emphasis on helping their people be the best are going to be viewed as better places to work than those who don't.

Please keep it flexible

Some managers argue that in a complex world, simplicity is the Holy Grail. Not so. Luckily, technology comes to the rescue. We can and must be able to treat people as individuals. Difficult if you have 10,000 employees, but not impossible. Just think about it. 10,000 people, 10,000 individuals all with their own lifestyle defining who they are and who they are at work. Since people do not leave their lifestyle behind when they get to work, they bring it with them. We need to find the ways to encourage that, not eradicate it. We need to celebrate it and – why ever not – use it for the good of the individual and the company.

Getting engaged:[7] *The Cargill story*

Cargill Incorporated is an international processor, marketer and distributor of agricultural, food, financial and industrial products and services, with 97,000 employees in 59 countries. A privately held company, it comprises more than 100 business units.

Recently, Cargill began a corporate transformation, centred on changing from a commodity products-oriented company to an integrated food products and food services company – from a supplier of ingredients to a provider of solutions. To do that they needed to create an environment where innovation fostered customer solutions. In support of this Cargill made changes in their organisational structure, compensation programmes and people processes. In addition, Cargill took a serious look at organisational behaviour, benchmarking a group of companies that threw up compelling evidence that to succeed as a customer solution provider they would have to excel at employee engagement.

Convinced of the correlation between employee engagement and business results, Cargill made 'engaged employees' one of four corporate-wide performance measures, along with satisfied customers, enriched communities and profitable growth.

Cargill partnered with Hewitt Associates to pilot an employee engagement study in four separate business units, totalling 7,500 employees. Following the successful pilot, Cargill then worked with Hewitt to conduct an engagement study of 25,000 salaried and some hourly employees around the world. The survey – translated into 27 languages – was administered partly on paper and partly over the Internet to meet the needs of Cargill's diverse employee population.

Gathering data from so many employees in so many places was a challenge for Cargill. Although the company originally intended to survey only a sampling of employees, management later decided to make the survey available to all 97,000. They wanted all employees to know that their opinion and their engagement matters.

Once the results were processed, managers could review the data, communicate it to employees and create an action plan within four weeks. Each business unit leader was held accountable for employees' perceptions of whether engagement results were shared and whether actions were taken based on those results. Hewitt and Cargill also built an on-line reporting system that allowed managers to view and model the data for their employees on-line anytime.

The engagement survey data has prompted some Cargill business units to redesign their compensation programmes and establish individual recognition systems. Others have made leadership changes or enhanced their career development programmes and several have improved communication between senior management and employees. Although the engagement survey is a tool provided at the corporate level, action plans must be developed and implemented at the business unit level, or even for each location, to be effective. With a diverse range of employees, raging from future traders in Geneva to plantation workers in Indonesia and meat packers in Kansas, different things engage employees in different cultures in different parts of the world.

The employee engagement concept enjoys tremendous support from Cargill's senior management. This support encourages co-operation from HR managers around the world, so that employee engagement is viewed as a business strategy not an HR programme. Although Cargill is still determining how their employee engagement efforts will impact the business overall, they believe that this work will allow them to achieve sustained business results, lower turnover and increased retention of the right people. Cargill believe that it will help them maintain a ready pool of qualified people to

promote as the company grows as well as helping employees understand that what they do as individuals impacts the company's business results.

Getting engaged: the Herman Miller story
During 2003 I paid a site visit to one of the most amazing companies
I have ever come across. Herman Miller make office furniture. Not
only that, they make it in a place called Zeeland Michigan, the heart-
land of the furniture industry established by Dutch settlers two cen-
turies ago. Until two years ago the firm was in hearty health. Then
recession hit. Large numbers of employees were made redundant. A
difficult thing to do when your main site is one of the region's major
employers and you are employing three generations of a family in
some cases.

But Herman Miller came through those travails incredibly well.
First by treating those that had to depart with respect, understanding and a great job-seeking package. But they also managed –
despite the toughest economic times the company had ever seen – to
keep the employees engaged.

Now, I have to be fair in this. They are not in the middle of a major
metropolis. They are, as our American cousins say, 'deep in the boon-
docks'. But maybe they should take credit for that too. Because in
wild, remote, unsophisticated Zeeland, Michigan (where Harry Potter
books got banned in school for their 'black magic' content) they have
not only engaged with their employees, they have taken that extra
step and put 'who they [the employees] are' into the workplace contract.

Their corporate brochure opens with the words, 'Cathedrals celebrate the idea of the heavens. Courthouses celebrate the concept of
justice. We believe workplaces can celebrate the process of work.' But
then they go on to say, 'The days we spend. The stories we tell. The
beliefs we share. The insights we seek. The blurred line between our
work "in here" and our lives "out there".'

You see, Herman MIller get it. They realise that everyone has their
own lifestyle and they bring it to work with them every day. And,
being in the middle of nowhere, the employees of Herman Miller are
the modern day equivalent of the American pioneer. They are
hunters, fishers, hikers, canoeists, campers and part-time ecologists.
When they came to work at Herman Miller, they brought their
lifestyle with them – it's still there!
Here's how they tell it.

In 1981 when Herman Miller built its Energy Center at the request of a group of employees, we only wanted to save money on electricity bills and stop sending so much scrap wood to the landfill. In 1989 another group of employees decided we needed to co-ordinate all the environmental work at Herman Miller. They formed the Environmental Quality Action Team and insisted that senior management get behind it. And senior management did.

Today, employees all over the company look for – and put into practice – new ways of becoming more environmentally aware. It's not a programme. It's part of corporate life.

There is only one thing wrong with this last statement. The programme is not part of corporate life. Corporate life at Herman Miller is a part of their employees' lifestyle(s).

In 1989, different groups of employees at Herman Miller discovered that their work on reducing waste, preventing harmful emissions, exploring safe materials and so on, had become a de facto environmental effort company-wide. They formed an Environmental Quality Action Team (EQAT), presented it to senior management, and included educating both customers and employees in their mission. EQAT continues its grassroots work today, represented by over 300 people on nine different sub-teams.

The deep-seated engagement of its employees has kept Herman Miller on track through the bad times. Not only has it won many awards for its environmental stance, it has actively kept on pushing the envelope of what is possible. They now have moved to their own vision of the future – sustainable capitalism – using materials at a rate slower than the natural environment can provide them for future generations.

But it is all delivered through the people who come to work each day. People who have a rich natural heritage and an appreciation of the environment around them. In one of their pieces of literature they say that employees come together each day 'in the spirit of a small city, where the important industries are new ideas, customer communication and employee collaboration.'

But most of all, they embrace the respect of the employee lifestyle, when they say, 'a place where work and people co-exist peacefully and constructively.'

Can you do what Herman Miller does in a different environment? After all their factory is surrounded by 37 acres of natural grasses, 6 acres of permanent wetlands and 5 acres of buffalo grasses and they adhere firmly to a policy of no lawn-mowing, no pesticides and no irrigation.

Yes you can. You just have to look for those 'keys' to what people bring with them every day. Maybe they are not all Davy Crockett's ancestors who know how to tree a squirrel, but people join companies because they feel affinity, and because they join others with similar views. So, in many cases, there are common ideals, causes and views that your employees share. If you want to engage them, find out what they are. For example many companies existing in the urban jungle have developed a tremendous level of staff engagement through volunteer programmes in local communities or charities. Others have used sports-related activity to light a spark.

The people who come to your firm come for a reason. After a week or so, they know – even if they need the job only until a better offer comes up – if they can 'be themselves here.' Can they bring themselves to your office everyday without checking in their lifestyle and personality at the front gate? If you engage them, fine. If you can – like Herman Miller – let them lead you to a better world, why would you try and make it difficult for them to do it?

Getting engaged: times of change at Safeway[8]
With annual sales of around £9 billion and 85,000 employees, Safeway is one of the UK's top grocery retailers. Recently, it has been the target of a heated take-over battle in the supermarket sector. This is a time when you really find out how well engaged your people are. Safeway not only came through, they probably increased rather then lessened the engagement quotient in the business. A large part of that was achieved through letting people be themselves, and do the things they did best. Let them bring 'themselves'.

On 9 January 2003, it was announced that Safeway had received a take-over bid from Morrisons, a Bradford-based supermarket group. Most employees experienced the typical change responses of shock, denial and blame. However, within days other supermarkets began expressing an interest in Safeway and it soon became clear that it could be a very protracted process, particularly when the government called for a full investigation by the Competition Commission. Safeway quickly realised that they needed a strategy to retain people and maintain motivation and morale in the long term.

The firm introduced financial incentives to encourage people to stay but also recognised that most staff at Safeway have a relational psychological contract, in that they are long serving and not motivated simply by money. The average length of service is 15 years for management and 9 years for the organisation as a whole. Safeway knew that it would have to appeal to people in different ways.

The approach the company developed therefore had two main aspects – transactional and relational. The latter element contained strategies for dealing with training and development, leadership, communication and morale and motivation. Rather than turning off training and development, because of uncertainty about the future, the firm invested far more into helping people prepare for the future, cope with the uncertainty and develop their skills. This has been a real 'wow' for employees and many have since reported that it had the single biggest impact upon their decision to stay. Safeway also revised their model of leadership behaviour, to help leaders manage the more relational aspects of their role more effectively in times of extreme uncertainty. The model, based around providing direction, gaining commitment and driving results was refocused to put it in the context of their current situation. This was supported by the introduction of a development programme to communicate and embed the required behaviours across the company's leadership teams.

Clear and frequent communication was vital. Safeway set up an area on its intranet called 'Our Future', to keep people informed of new developments. They had a 'Meeting For Everyone', at least every four weeks at their Hayes head office where board members present the current situation and open the floor to questions. This was video linked to distribution depots and regional offices, and phone linked to all store managers so people nationwide could gain access and ask questions. Safeway also established 'Colleague Councils' ahead of legislation, where staff representatives met senior people for two-way dialogue, the outcomes being cascaded throughout the organis-ation. They also had a strong emphasis on encouraging social events and fun activities in order to create a sense of team camaraderie.

Considering the uncertainty, Safeway has reported that it main-tained a very creditable business performance and experienced no significant change in labour turnover, with it even falling in some parts of the business. This has amazed onlookers, especially in the media, who were speculating that they would haemorrhage staff.

Another measure is the customer service programme Friendliest Store in Town. This is a monthly measure of the service customers receive in Safeway stores and is independently validated by an exter-nal organisation using mystery shoppers. Since January 2003, it shows that the company consistently improved its performance every month.

Removing fear of an uncertain future was great management, but using the inherent commitment of employees and feeding that through improved training, development and social events, underscores that Safeway understand that employees are themselves at work, not what we compel them to be.

Getting engaged: the Savoy Group story
The hotel industry is notorious for labour turnover. In fact the industry average in Europe and the US hovers between 70 and 80 per cent annually. Traditionally, this has been blamed on poor pay and conditions and the fact that the hotel and catering industries are often the first foot on the ladder for many employees just beginning their working lives.

Sara Edwards, now Group Director of HR at the Savoy Group (that includes such prestigious London luxury spots as Claridge's, The Connaught, Simpson's-in-the-Strand and The Savoy itself), was convinced that sky-high turnover didn't have to happen. 'Just managing employee churn isn't good for the business or for our customers, many of whom are regulars and want to see continuity of service,' she says, 'so we set out to change that.'

What Sara Edwards and her team did – first at Claridge's and later throughout the group, was to treat people differently, engage them and give them pride in the contribution they were making. 'Yes, we do pay well for our industry,' admits Edwards, 'but that is not what our staff stay for. In our surveys the top score is for "recognition and value" which last time rated out at 99.2 per cent. People stay with us because they feel valued.'

Does it work, in retaining staff? Enthuses Edwards 'When we began our programme, turnover at Claridge's was 73 per cent. Last year it was 27 per cent and so far this year (2004) to end May it was 10.4 per cent.'

Much of what the Savoy Group have done is simply to make people feel wanted. There is a free chiropody clinic (hotel staff are on their feet a lot); a full-time occupational therapist; health adviser and an osteopath, which staff can attend in work time. Each hotel has a separate staff restaurant with its own chefs. 'This is important so that people get proper, cooked meals, not what a busy chef, whose priority is the paying customer, has the time to do,' explains Edwards, 'and it is free to everyone.' Now the group is looking at introducing yoga lessons for staff.

Edwards stresses that the other factor in helping to reduce dramatically the turnover rates is open, honest communication. 'When 9/11 happened we knew we would have problems – there were hundreds of cancellations within hours – so we gathered all the staff together in the ballroom and told them what we were going to do.' Edwards continues, 'Then we met again the next day and weekly thereafter. We knew it would be a difficult time but we used it to retrain lots of staff into new jobs and there was a great team spirit.'

Edwards and her team also asked staff to tell them what were their hobbies and interests or other skills so that they could identify other work opportunities for people.

But the one thing that gives Edwards most satisfaction is probably her introduction of what they call the 'Going for Gold' programme. 'We have the usual employee of the month programme,' says Edwards, 'but what we wanted was something that was instant. Something that could reward immediately, was low cost to operate, but had high value for the employee (managers were also included in the programme).'

The 'Going for Gold' initiative is based on seven key service values, and managers award instant gold cards to employees who demonstrate them. It may be excellent service to a customer, or a great idea. Whatever it is, the reward is instant. The employee gets the card and then goes to the HR department where there is a pot of 'gold' (mainly gold covered chocolate money!). In the pot are 32 envelopes (renewed monthly). In each enveloped is a prize. These range from a limousine to take you home after your shift to an extra day off, a lie-in or a dinner out with your partner. Top prize – each month – is a night's stay, dinner and breakfast in one of the penthouses (£3,850 a night rooms) with your partner. Only rule, the prize must be taken within four weeks.

'The great thing,' smiles Edwards, 'is that everyone knows about it. And because it is open to everyone it is really an exciting programme that does get all of us involved.'

Edwards believes that every firm in every industry can do the same sort of thing. 'Often people say to me, "well that's easy for you in your industry," but I don't agree. If anyone bothers to think for a while, this type of engagement programme can be applied anywhere.'

KEY ISSUES

- A need to recognise that the working world isn't the same as even five years ago.
- Lifestyle is the number one issue for the smart new-age employee.
- People want to be themselves at work and we need to cater for that.
- Work/life balance doesn't cut it – LIFE/WORK balance does.
- Engagement is the golden word for employees. Attaining it is like finding the pot of gold at the end of the rainbow – extremely difficult.
- Flexibility in workstyle and workplace are already paramount.
- Flexibility itself needs to adapt constantly as the lifestyles of individual employees change due to their evolving circumstances.
- Age plays an increasingly significant part in how different groups develop – we need to manage that.
- Workplaces will have to meet – and even exceed – the wants and expectations of employees.
- Increasingly, relocation to a new job or company will be a family-driven decision.
- Wellness programmes are set to increase as employees seek to make their workplace an ever-healthier environment.
- Reward structures will have to be flexible too – adapting to meet the changing compensation requirement of an individual employee.

Notes

1   TOWERS PERRIN (2003) *Working Today: Understanding What Drives Employee Engagement.*

2   (2000) *Funky Business: Talent Makes Capital Dance.* Pearson Education.

3   (1997) *Teleworking in Brief.* Butterworth Heinemann.

4   (2002) *Talent Magnet.* Financial Times/Pearson Education.

5   (January 2004) *Catalyst Health and Fitness survey.* HR Gateway.

6   (September 2003) Aon Consulting Global Forum.

7 *Getting engaged: the Cargill story* is based on material extracted from *Hewitt Magazine*, the corporate publication of Hewitt Associates, (2003) Vol 6, Issue 2.

8 *Getting engaged: times of change at Safeway* is adapted from the report (2003) *Managing on the Edge, Psychological Contracts in Transition*. Roffey Park Management Centre.

Chapter 5

Great employees!
... Where?

A lot of leaders want people to feel good about them.
Great leaders get people feeling good about
themselves.

Shay McConnon

A great deal of talent is lost in the world for want of a
little courage. Every day sends to their graves obscure
men who timidity prevented from making a first
effort; who, if they could have been induced to begin,
would in all probability gone to great lengths in the
career of fame. The fact is, to do anything in the world
worth doing, we must not stand back shivering and
thinking of the cold and danger, but jump in a
scramble through as well as we can.

Sydney Smith

Throughout this book we have made one big assumption: that you
want to hire the best and brightest. Now, having established that this
is possible if you allow them into your world on their terms and not
yours, let's take a look at just what the criteria for engaging
employees are. In the last chapter we talked about letting people be
themselves at work and of the necessity to be flexible in thought and
action. Now let's look at some of the expectations of the best and
brightest. And remember, the brighter the people, the more they are
going to invest the job you give them with their own lifestyle and
their own expectations.

The wonders of the worldwide web

They will begin their relationship with you by checking out your reputation – in depth. The worldwide web may be a wonderful thing, but it means that all our businesses are essentially transparent. Even if we as employers don't put that much information on our corporate website there is someone, somewhere, who can be relied on to know all about us (or to provide their highly personalised version), and where prospective candidates – and curious employees who need more information than management wants to give – can get the low-down. Executive search professionals will tell you that in today's information-overloaded world, many candidates just say 'no' on the basis of checking out a website. If they don't like how the company looks then that is as far as they'll go.

Get your website right

So I suppose the first point of contact in getting people engaged is holding their attention for a while. And this means that your external website, and the hard copy materials with which you support it, need to be geared toward the types of people you want to attract: a corporate version of the age-old mating dance. Put it this way, go look at some internet sites and you will quickly see what I mean. Some are turn-offs, some are turn-ons, and many are obviously the personal hobby of some freak in the IT department.

I used to advise managers to call their company's main switchboard number when they were out of town to see what the welcome was like. That *was* the first point of contact with the firm. Now go check out your website, because that is where prospective employees begin. From the appearance of some of them it is clear no senior manager has clicked on for some time.

And really think through who you are trying to reach. If you are an insurance firm there probably isn't much point getting too far out. If you are in new media, well 'just do it' as they say. But never forget that you need to leave an impression of your business and the kinds of people who would feel welcome in that environment. You don't get a second chance with this.

Just assume that by the time you get to meet any candidate they'll know a lot more about you than any job seeker would have even five years ago. The bright ones will have done their research almost as well as a Wall Street analyst.

Looking for a real fit

Psychologist Elisabeth Marx, who works for the London-based search firm Hanover Fox, and author of *Breaking Through Culture Shock*, says that candi-

> 'They are also driven to a company by the uniqueness of the culture and how they perceive the mood. Basically, how will they and their expectations fit in.'

dates today 'look more for a real fit with the individuals they will work with, and particularly the boss they work for.' She adds, 'They are also driven to a company by the uniqueness of the culture and how they perceive the mood. Basically, how will they and their expectations fit in.'

Marx also observes that other factors play far more in the candidate's decision to join any business. 'Most smart candidates are not interested in instant gratification,' she explains, 'they are not concerned about stability, money, or instant success. They ask one question, "will it enhance my career – long term?"'

The other thing that Marx has observed as a critical sea change in the marketplace is that 'people look to join companies with a strong brand image. In 1999 they'd go anywhere if the money was right – not now.' In all this there has been a real seismic shift in the tectonic plates of employment and employee engagement, reversing in many cases the fine footwork of the mating dance. Candidates choose companies, not the other way around. There is little hint of sweaty-palmed interviews and landing a job at any price.

Two favourite quotes from a UK electronics industry executive and a US automotive vice-president, which indicate how much the recruitment process has changed:

- 'I think prospective employees still ask the same questions, they just listen a whole lot closer to the answers.'
- 'Prospective employees know a whole lot more about your business than they ever did. They are going to ask you, "Why did these people leave? What are your plans for this division?" Five years ago no one would ever have asked these type of questions.'

Don't oversell

This can lead to one of the great recruitment bear traps, the tendency to oversell the job in the hope of snaring the candidate. In the heady days of the late 1990s this was a regular occurrence. It is not a good idea. Any smart new employee will quickly realise that they have been 'sold' the wrong deal, which means that the whole recruitment process has to begin again. Don't fall into this trap, it really isn't worth it, no matter how much you want the candidate to join up. Remember, if we agree that the person who is going to join you is bringing his lifestyle to your business, when he finds it not only doesn't fit now, but never will, he or she will be gone all too quickly.

Say 'hi' to the alumni

Richard Savage, former head of HR at market research giant A.C. Nielsen, and now an organisational consultant linked to the FutureWork Forum, has a great trick up his sleeve to sway the dithering candidate who is not sure whether to join up or jump off – wheel in an ex-employee. 'This is more powerful than any would-be co-worker,' advises Savage, 'it sends a powerful message that if this ex-employee is still prepared to say what a good time they had – even after they have left – and the company is happy to let them do that, then it must be a pretty open place to work.'

I know what you did last summer

Another tip from a seasoned professional: Tom Acuff, managing director for Europe, Africa, Middle East for search firm DHR International notes that where you are hiring freshly-minted MBAs, 'it's often impossible to slide a sheet of paper between them, they are so similar in their qualifications – in fact you can have a whole group that are essentially clones of each other.' Acuff's solution to this dilemma of who to hire is, 'Forget the academic record, and see what they did in their downtime. If they did nothing, well, that lets them out, if they climbed Mount Everest that's pretty enterprising, but if they interned every summer at Goldman Sachs, you just might want to hire the guy.' This is one of the few chances you get these days to get candidate selection back under your control, rather than theirs. Just one point on this: if you happen to be running an outdoor clothing company or you are L.L. Bean, pick the guy who climbed Everest, won't you! I really cannot emphasise this enough, the candidate is bringing himself or herself with them – if an Everest climber fits your culture, take them.

Ability to change jobs

Another issue that has been coming up increasingly in candidate interviews is 'Can I change jobs, or even pursue an alternative career if I want to without leaving the company?' A lot of companies are not geared up even to answer the question, never mind deliver on it. But it does make sense to think about it, because rather than lose someone who doesn't like what they are doing – and doesn't identify with the role – you can allow them to move internally to a job that reflects that lifestyle of theirs (or the new lifestyle they have recently acquired, possibly through getting married or having children). One professional services company, Deloitte and Touche, had a huge shock some years ago when they developed an electronic job vacancy board and 40 per cent of the staff applied for new jobs in the first 48 hours. Again this underscores the lifestyle need to be yourself at work. Often people's lifestyles change, but the job doesn't. All you get then are bored, unproductive and increasingly restless and resentful employees. Very often, people leave a company to go and do a totally different job in another company when they probably – if anyone had bothered – could have been easily accommodated without taking the drastic decision to quit. When you consider the

> When you consider the cost of recruitment, asking people if their own personal needs are being fulfilled at performance review time, and being able to do something about it if they are not, would be a great idea.

cost of recruitment, asking people if their own personal needs are being fulfilled at performance review time, and being able to do something about it if they are not, would be a great idea.

Don't make mobility a condition

While many people cite international travel as a prerequisite for taking a job (at least until they find out how much fun it really isn't), there are others who shun the concept of being moved around at an employer's whim. Indeed, the prevailing wisdom is that the mobility issue (or lack of a will to be mobile) is one of the biggest problems facing cross-border operating companies today. Working spouses and a desire not to disturb a child's schooling are usually cited as the top reasons for wanting to stay put. Therefore, smart recruiters are not trying to lay down the condition that employees need to be mobile. Anyway, thanks to today's communication technology it is possible to stay in one place your entire career and manage remote teams (possibly with site visits on a regular basis). Once again this refusal to move just because an employer wants you to plays straight into the hands of the 'being myself' argument. A decade or so ago, managers would gladly up sticks, with their family trailing behind (hence the term trailing spouses) and no questions asked. Those old enough to recall IBM in its hey-day of the 1970s will recall that the acronym didn't just stand for International Business Machines, but 'I've Been Moved.'

A lot has changed since those days. Professionals tend to partner with other professionals. Today there is less likelihood than ever before of them just simply agreeing to a national or continental move just because the other partner's firm has requested it. People put down roots and their lifestyle becomes part of that stability. Unless there are good reasons to want to change that lifestyle and try another, there are fewer and fewer reasons these days for moving. This means that to attract the right kind of talent into a business, managers have to find other solutions. Of course there will always be managers whose lifestyle option is crafted around the idea of moving every few years. They – and very often their spouse too – find these 'adventures' exciting and very fulfilling. They are who they are. Not only do they eagerly embrace a new geography and a new work challenge, they totally revel in it. These people are – and will continue to be – like gold dust. When you find them put them quickly on your 'most endangered species' list. Really, do it. These people should be protected by the World Wildlife Fund. They are rare beasts and should be treated as such.

Then again, the other tendency is to find that an unwillingness to be highly mobile is something that develops over time. Again it is about lifestyle choices. Young, single people often crave new experiences and are eager to travel and discover new opportunities, places and cultures. As we age, our horizons don't necessarily narrow, but they do mature. We put down roots, we become more firmly tied to a place or places that reflect who we are and what we want to be (and work is only a part of that). So again, employees need to be understood and encouraged for what they can contribute at different times in their lives. They change, we must change too if we are to accommodate them and use their talents in the best possible way.

Take on the risk

This is something I have been advocating for years, whether the conditions are boom or bust. Too many good people have been lost from
organisations because they were denied an opportunity of promotion or
of a new assignment when they knew they were ready, but the company
did not. Those words, 'You're doing a great job Sally, but let's review
your next step in another 12 months,' might sound reasonable to a
manager. But it translates to Sally as, 'We really don't think you are
good enough for that promotion/assignment, maybe we'll look at it
again in a year or so.' Sally goes home, the headhunter calls and it's all
over bar the leaving party.

As several senior managers who 'get it' have told me, 'Your concerns
about moving them up are never matched by the company that wants
to hire them. "Use them or lose them" becomes the watchword.'

Having said that, there is the opposite risk too. Pushing too hard
and forcing someone to stretch the envelope of experience and responsibility beyond where they are really comfortable – making the workstyle
you have chosen dominate the employee's lifestyle. This is almost
always bound to fail. The employee will be under pressure (pressure
that he or she has not created and is not in control of), and their performance will consequently suffer. When lifestyle and workstyle get
into conflict, instead of co-existing there has to be a breakdown somewhere. Often this situation occurs because senior managers (with successful careers under their belt) fail to grasp the fact that not everyone
wants to be promoted or manage others. They are very, very happy
doing a job they like. They are committed, engaged and most often
respect the firm for allowing them to do what they want – live their
lifestyle inside your workstyle. To meddle with that is to court disaster.
This does mean that developing different career tracks inside a business
makes a lot of sense, so you can accommodate all those different
lifestyles that people bring to work with them every day. Accommodate
your employees' lives (think back to that table in Chapter 1) by getting
what you want and what they want into synergy. It *is* possible to have
their goals and your goals running in parallel.

Dealing with the diversity question

Ah diversity! Ask 10 managers to define diversity and you'll get a
dozen different responses (two of them will give more than one answer

and if you don't believe me go out in the corridor now and start asking the question). Employee diversity is a hot potato, a flavour of the year, a coming trend. Managers I talk to say that without developing the skills to hire and nurture a diverse workforce they will not have enough talent to survive. This, by all accounts, is true.

However, most companies seem unclear what 'diversity' means. To my mind it means opening up your organisation to new streams of talent. Hiring from different skill sets and different geographies. It can also mean an avowed intent to, for example, increase the percentage of women in supervisory and managerial roles within a business.

This then means that you have to be able quickly and easily to integrate these people into your business. If you are already having a hard time with engaging your present employee line-up that's going to be an uphill task. But most senior HR professionals will tell you that we do need to spread the search for new recruits to an ever-greater degree. In recent months, I have heard of two companies, one a leading banking firm, the other a professional services business, that have appointed senior-level executives to the exclusive role of looking for both mature and emerging talent, anywhere in the world. This is going to be one of the great recruitment battles of the next 10 years.

In recruiting from a diverse set of skills and geographies we are going to have to be much more open to different lifestyles than we are today. Maybe, many of us will struggle with this, but if we hold the central thought that the people we recruit are bringing their lifestyle to work, then we can be successful. Especially so, if we realise that their lifestyle will most probably change quickly as they embrace new experiences and a new cultural setting.

> *In recruiting from a diverse set of skills and geographies we are going to have to be much more open to different lifestyles than we are today.*

What makes an employee engaged?

You've hired your new employee. So why is he or she going to stay? Well there are a huge variety of reasons why they will do that. What I have been able to do in researching for this book is narrow down the factors that engage an employee and will contribute to their longer-term commitment.[1] Does anyone do all these things? I don't think so. I think many excellent companies recognise what the criteria for engagement and commitment are, but find it practically impossible to have all these operating at 100 per cent efficiency at the same time, 24 hours a day, seven days a week, 365 days a year.

After a great deal of discussion with senior managers, below is my employee engagement 'wish-list'. I am sure it isn't exhaustive and it isn't set out with any kind of priority or importance. Hopefully it will give you some ideas of the issues you need to address to drive talent to your door and keep it when you get it.

The employee engagement wish-list

- lifestyle/workstyle balance and flexibility
- excellent leadership at top
- work with industry leader
- work with inspirational people (boss)
- work on 'hot' projects
- work with leading customers and suppliers
- opportunity to lead others
- recognition of ideas
- excellent work environment (location/facilities)
- international opportunity (travel)
- receiving positive feedback
- company-sponsored education
- financial rewards (salary/bonus)
- flexible benefits
- healthcare programme
- sabbaticals.

Let's look at these individually, and see what we as employers need to do to make them work.

Lifestyle/workstyle balance and flexibility

We've covered this key criterion in some detail earlier in the book. However, I believe that this is the starting point for everything. Subscribe to lifestyle/workstyle approach and the other issues flow from that. Everyone knows the story that a company's greatest asset walks out of the door every day at six o'clock and might come back the following day. When employees leave your office at six o'clock they are hopefully committed to coming back the following morning. If their lifestyle and your workstyle are synchronised, then they will.

Excellent leadership at the top

Smart people only need a few days to establish whether the top management know what's going on. And smart people go to work and engage with other smart people. If you've got smart top managers, celebrate; if you've got a lousy group at the top of the tree, you won't keep the best talent for very long. It all comes down to respect. If employees respect the leadership you have won a major victory in the battle for engagement and commitment. And never underestimate the power a charismatic leader has to engage people. People – I most certainly believe – follow great leaders. I mean, think about it, no one ever said, 'I'm off to join the ABC company, I hear they have a great executive committee.' Well they don't, do they?

Work with industry leader

Yes, everyone likes to be associated with a successful organisation. If you are successful it pays to let the marketplace know about it – you'll attract and keep talented individuals.

Work with inspirational people (and bosses)

Work colleagues can make or break a lifestyle/workstyle choice. If employees work well together, spark off ideas in each other, that's great. If they don't, that lifestyle/workstyle equation gets called into question. 'Can I ever be happy in this place?' is not the sort of question you want employees asking themselves. The same test applies to the immediate superior. It has long been said that people join companies and leave bosses. How true, especially if their boss changes. This can be one of the biggest turn-offs, quickly and totally destroying the lifestyle/workstyle equation of the individual.

Work on 'hot' projects

This is another of those key engagement factors. Great projects grab people's attention, fire them up and are an effective way to provoke total engagement. I recall years ago visiting the Alstom TGV plant in France. All the engineers were *so* enthusiastic. As one explained to me, 'for an engineer this *is* the place. We are working on the biggest, fastest machine on land.' You got the impression they would work 24 hours a day if they could, and for free too!

Work with leading customers and suppliers

Smart employees want to learn and develop their skills. Often the best places to do this are with customers and suppliers. Being given opportunities to experience this again are part of an ongoing engagement process.

Opportunity to lead others

This is perhaps not for everyone, but it is on the 'wish list' of many. And, as I pointed out earlier, it usually pays to take on the risk and give someone an opportunity to push the career envelope to its maximum. Remember, don't look at the issue from your perspective, consider the employee's view, and their lifestyle/workstyle view of themselves. This is a moment when people are highly vulnerable and at a pivotal cross-roads. They could be given the chance and fail. Or they could succeed. Or they could be told to wait, get frustrated and leave. The lifestyle/workstyle equation comes under great strain at this time.

Recognition of ideas

Make sure that the 'idea factory' in your business runs smoothly and give recognition for people's ideas. This is a crucial factor in stimulating engagement from employees. Don't give the recognition and the ideas quickly dry up. Worse still, people will take them elsewhere instead.

Excellent work environment (location and facilities)

As I have already explained, you can put the most beautiful office facility in the wrong place and no one will work there. The work environment begins with the location and the ease of getting there. And yes, the internal facilities need to be in place to feed those lifestyle/workstyle needs. For example, some employees don't mind working late if they know there is a take-away they can access, or a bistro or bar they can use. Equally, smart companies that seek to ease the domestic drudgery of their employees win out. Laundry, dry-cleaning services, auto service drop-offs, video rental, medical, dental and supermarket shopping services on-site all help to keep employees engaged and not concerned about other issues while at work. On the subject of environment, my favourite example is the service management company in Denmark who have a company dog who spends work hours at reception. If employees get stressed the idea is that they take the dog for a walk in the woods around the building.

International opportunity (travel)

Gaining experience through cross-border work is a great turn-on for many. Being able to travel and experience first-hand how others execute their work is a vital component of a job. However, Monday to Friday travel week after week takes its toll. So when employees say they want to travel, put that into the lifestyle/workstyle context and get the balance right.

Receiving positive feedback

Everyone knows this is critical, but our new-age employees have a higher level of expectation. The biggest concern here is whether we all have enough well-trained managers to ensure that the process really works.

Company-sponsored education

This is a catch-all that covers everything from Harvard's Executive Summer School, to specialist technical courses and personal coaching and mentoring. In most cases these days employees don't really see these as 'nice-to-haves' but 'must-haves'. However, with the dearth of training and development these past years, companies are going to find themselves playing – and paying for – catch-up processes if they truly want to send a serious message about people development.

Financial rewards (salary, bonus, benefits)

These really go without saying. But as explained earlier, many companies are not overhauling and re-tuning their compensation systems and strategies quickly enough to meet changing market conditions. There is no doubt that we are going to have to move toward *flexible benefits* if we are to genuinely tap into the lifestyle/workstyle equation of our people. The only way we can do that is to come up with some innovative ideas to embrace their needs. Similarly, smart managers are concerned to provide a robust *healthcare programme*. Companies determined to leave the onus for this with the individual employee are going to have to fight yet another competitive advantage from those companies who provide it. In the end, choice of a firm to work with may not come down to one single criterion, but to several varied criteria, all just that little bit better or more flexible in one company than another.

A good example of that would be the last item on the Employee Engagement Wish-list: *sabbaticals*. In truth, virtually no one offers them, but those who do gain a certain distinction from other companies. Smart companies, I have observed, who offer this usually don't leave it as an open-ended 'vacation', but set the employee the task of studying, developing some blue-sky ideas or working on a special assignment (possibly with a not-for-profit or educational organisation).

Leading those lifestyle/workstyle revolutionaries

We are now beginning to understand a great deal about what these new-age employees expect and the criteria that fire up their ability and willingness to engage with one company as opposed to another. But what does this mean for the manager who has to make it all come together? The line manager who has to make sure that he relates to those lifestyle/workstyle needs of his individual employees.

During the course of writing this book, a close colleague of mine, psychologist Shay McConnon, the founder of People First (www.PeopleFirst-Intl.com) and one of the world's leading lecturers on motivation, negotiation and conflict resolution, produced some ideas around how we perceive each other in a work-related environment. I was so impressed, I begged him to let me use some of this material. He, being a truly kind man, said, 'Go ahead.' What follows are essentially Shay McConnon's ideas wrapped up in some of my own words.

Shay McConnon's key concept is that we all have our own views and these are the ones that tend to dominate how we operate and how we view others. Getting through that and looking at things in a different way is a key part of beginning to understand the lifestyle/workstyle of others, all of us – including *you*.

Consider this dialogue:

'How would you know you were a good team leader?' I asked Pete.

'Have a compelling vision and then inspire and empower the team to achieve it' he replied.

'Whose criteria are those?'

'Mine, I suppose.'

'What are the criteria of your team members, what do you need to be doing so they would consider you a good team leader?'

'Not so sure, probably the same as mine.'

'Would you like to find out?'

'OK.'

Imagine then flushing out Pete's team's real, personal criteria, and finding many differences. Criteria that were important to some, were not to others. Pete was surprised that some did not want their hearts won – that concept had little meaning for them. Others did not want their minds won.

As the discussion went on amongst the team, it became clear what a difficult job Pete had if he was to meet the criteria of his team members and be accepted by all as a 'good' leader. Things became even more complicated when we assembled the criteria of Pete's boss and his criteria for considering Pete a good or bad team leader.

The lesson to learn is that we cannot generalise on what makes a good leader, or on why minds and hearts are won. Leadership is person specific. What is critical to one person will not be for another. Some people are turned off by the outgoing, dynamic, high energy, charismatic style of leadership, but for every one of those there are 'quiet' leaders in the workplace who have many followers making real differences.

Effective leadership

The most effective style of leadership would appear to be related to the personalities of those being lead, and what best fits with their lifestyle/workstyle notions. People follow because their criteria are met. Leaders need to measure themselves against the criteria of their people rather than the textbook or the expert criteria; they need to engage with the individual's view of the world. Successful leaders know the criteria of their people. They have fluency and flexibility in their leadership style. They individualise rather than generalise.

Successful leaders know the criteria of their people. They have fluency and flexibility in their leadership style. They individualise rather than generalise.

Management and leadership

You manage systems, budgets, and time, but you lead people. Leadership is about the people side of things. It is about rapport, communication, loyalty, creating engagement and respect, helping people believe in themselves and inspiring them to higher levels of performance within their own lifestyle criteria.

Leaders need to understand people and the dynamics of behaviour. They need to understand what motivates people and how they can be inspired, excited and moved to action within the boundaries of their very personal lifestyle/workstyle balance. They need to understand that while people react to the values, beliefs and behaviours of the leader, they respond in different ways depending on the lifestyle/workstyle expectations of the individual.

We are dramatically different

The single biggest mistake people, and hence leaders, make in their relationships is to assume that people are like them, have similar needs and values and would like to be treated as they would. People are dramatically different, so different it is as if they are from different planets. The criteria for winning minds and hearts can differ widely from person to person.

In Shay McConnon's view, there are three key personality types: carers, doers, and thinkers. Basically, every one of us is one, or a combination, of these types, and the mix of qualities defines how each needs to be treated.

Carers

These people value caring over achieving or getting things right. They are thoughtful, loyal, generous people who like to be accommodating. Usually they are good listeners and show a genuine interest in other people and their issues. They don't like conflict and work hard at keeping harmony in the team.

Expect them to want a personal relationship with you and to value you for who you are.

Leaders recognise that the values driving such behaviours will centre around partnership, teamwork, two-way communication, sincerity and harmony. Leaders need to appeal to these lifestyle values with this group if they are to inspire action and get business results.

Typically, these people will want their hearts won, not their minds. The leader wins their hearts by his humanity and approachability. They need a leader to be friendly, likeable, supportive, empathetic and thoughtful – someone who remembers the 'little' things. In this way the heart is won, commitment and respect grow and productive action is inspired.

Conversely, they will find it hard to respect someone who is arrogant, pushy, bossy, selfish, sarcastic, anyone who excludes them or abuses their generosity, who invades their lifestyle/workstyle in a heavy-handed fashion. They feel particularly valued with opportunities genuinely to help others, when their support is recognised and when working for someone who is thoughtful.

Doers

They value achieving over caring or getting things right. These are assertive, high energy, no nonsense type of people who love to achieve and get things done. They usually have little time for small talk and like to get straight down to the business in hand. They like their information concise, 'one-minute manager' style. Bullet points and summaries often characterise this style. They don't appreciate their time being wasted.

Expect them to want a functional relationship with you and to value you for what you can do.

Leaders recognise that the values that drive such behaviours will centre on achievement, success, competence, efficiency, speed, status and winning. Leaders appeal to these lifestyle/workstyle values to inspire, motivate and persuade.

Doers typically need both their minds and hearts won. They need someone driving forward with passion. They will follow a leader who has an exciting vision, someone who is dynamic, future orientated and achievement driven. Conversely, they will find it hard to respect someone who is complacent, talks problems, wastes time or makes excuses. They feel particularly valued when asked to troubleshoot, to achieve against the odds, to fight deadlines, to face up to difficult challenges and when given responsibility.

Thinkers

Getting things right is more important to them than caring or being successful. They are fair, principled and usually risk averse. They tend to be prudent and would prefer not to make a decision than make a wrong one. They are the perfectionists of our world and are usually thorough in whatever they do.

Expect them to want an intellectual relationship with you and to value you for how much you know.

Leaders recognise that the lifestyle/workstyle values that drive such behaviours will centre on quality, integrity, logic, accuracy and independence. Leaders tap into to these values when they need to influence, persuade and get rapport.

Typically these people will want their minds won, not their hearts. Their minds are won by the leader's principles, integrity, accuracy and attention to detail.

They need a leader to be prudent, someone who respects systems and procedures and is concerned about standards. Conversely, they will find it hard to respect someone who is frivolous, ignores the problems, exaggerates, is over familiar, someone who insists a deadline is met at the expense of quality.

They feel particularly valued with opportunities to increase their knowledge base, when they can do the job properly and when they are given problems to solve.

While some people do fall 'cleanly' into one of these categories, many of us have combinations of these motivations. The criteria for winning minds and hearts will need to be very individualised to appeal to these 'mixed' lifestyle/workstyle values.

Motivation

Influential leaders know their people. They know the lifestyle/workstyle choices that drive the individual's behaviour and they appeal to these to create effective relationships. The leader recognises that to get people to do a worthwhile job he has to give them a worthwhile job to do. A worthwhile job will embody that person's core values.

By ensuring people have a worthwhile job the leader improves motivation and reduces the need for supervision. Comments like 'Well it is a job – it pays the mortgage,' indicate there is a lack of worth to be found in that job and that an individual's lifestyle needs are not being met or addressed.

The tail wag factor!

Money buys a dog but it is love (and food!) that makes it wag its tail. You might have high-quality people in your team but you may not be getting high-quality performances. If people are not being led

according to their own, highly personalised lifestyle/workstyle expectations you will not get the level of performance of which they are
capable.

Organisations are not successful, it is the people in those organisations who are. They drive it forward or put it into reverse. Dig deeply
into organisational problems and you will always get to people.
Conflict, stress, misunderstanding, poor communication, demotiv-
ation, resistance, low morale, all have their origins in people and their lifestyle needs not being met. These are leader-

Organisations are only as effective as the people in them. People are only as effective as their leaders enable them to be.

ship issues. Organisations are only as effective as the people in them.
People are only as effective as their leaders enable them to be.

Shay McConnon's famous chicken vindaloo recipe

As Shay McConnon says, 'Effective leaders avoid what I call the chicken
vindaloo trap – treating others as you want to be treated. I love chicken
vindaloo, but that is no reason to use it as bait when fishing! To be successful I must use what appeals to the fish – maggots – even if it
doesn't appeal to me. You will not win the heart of a carer using the
doer's leadership criteria. You will not win the thinker's mind using
caring criteria.'

Shay McConnon goes on to explain that, 'One day, in the middle of
one of my team-building sessions, the team leader apologised to the
rest of the team for constantly giving them challenges. "Challenges
light my fire," he said, "and I thought this worked for everyone". He
had been fishing with chicken vindaloo! That wasn't the bait that was
going to capture the hearts and minds of this group.'

Within this complex lifestyle/workstyle need structure are literally
millions of permutations. Some people are motivated by challenges,
others can feel 'used' by this same behaviour; not everyone needs to be
overtly appreciated; not everyone will be happy when you offer your
help. Even the end-of-year bonus doesn't work for everyone.

Effective leaders make great efforts to know their people and understand
how they need to be treated in order to add value and create worth. They
are approachable. They have open, collaborative lines of communication.

The leader may not be able to meet every one of an individual's
lifestyle/workstyle needs, as they will have restrictions and needs of
their own. However, the crucial thing is that people sense a willingness

from the leader to understand them and a knowledge that they would willingly meet their needs if it were possible. They give people what they don't normally get, which is why the leader gets from them what they don't normally give.

Ill-informed goodwill hurts business

The vast majority of managers are good people who work hard and have the best interest of the business and its people at heart. While they are likely to treat individual employees differently, often it is not in the appropriately different way. Again they fall into the chicken vindaloo trap, 'I delegate in the way I like to be delegated to. I give feedback in the way I like feedback given to me.' They think they are adding value in how they approach others but in fact, they may be doing the opposite – eroding value.

This is tragic and comes with a high cost to the business. It is tragic because the goodwill is there. The manager is trying to get it right. Organisations are full of good-willed managers who are getting it wrong, causing stress, de-motivation, low morale, and poor productivity. Studies show that 75 per cent of people leave jobs because of relationship issues and most of those are with the immediate supervisor. These managers are likely to be good-willed people, doing the best they can with the awareness they have. Ill-informed goodwill hurts the business.

People don't leave good leaders. Instead they are likely to follow them out of the organisation when they leave.

Developing leaders

People are often promoted to managerial positions because they are technically good. But in the multi-faceted organisational structures of the twenty-first century, this role requires new and complex skills of motivating, influencing and empowering. We don't inherit these skills, we are not taught them at school and many of our work models are inappropriate. Your company may be using state of the art information technology and yet managing its people on outdated principles of leadership psychology; stifling energy and creativity. In effect, wasting the human resource.

To create the leadership culture, where people feel understood, valued, respected and empowered, effectively meeting their lifestyle/workstyle needs involves creating a set of beliefs to support these behaviours. It means providing opportunities for people to understand the lifestyle value set of their colleagues and the skills to work respectfully with these differences.

Developing the manager's potential

Shay McConnon's arguments are not only correct, but – as I have insisted earlier – point to the fact that in these complex times we need to be sure that our managers are able to tap into the needs of the individual, understanding both the personal and professional needs. However, it is the chosen lifestyle that rules above all, so line managers in particular must gain the skills to understand how to engage their people by connecting with their overall life expectations. Only through doing that will we be able to build a strong engaged workforce. The difficulty, as has already been pointed out, is that many managers lack good people skills and understanding the motivations of your team is going to be harder than ever as we go forward. Well, no one ever said it was going to be easy.

> *it is the chosen lifestyle that rules above all, so line managers in particular must gain the skills to understand how to engage their people by connecting with their overall life expectations.*

In Chapter 6, we'll take a look at the issues surrounding corporate communications and why, if you want to enthuse and gain respect from those employees with their lifestyle/workstyle equation at the forefront of their day-to-day life, it is set to take on a new importance.

Raising the Jolly Roger

Often the people who have the 'keys' to knowledge in a business are unrecognised and certainly unrecorded. Every company has them. They are the people who cross the usual lines of corporate demarcation and they are the people who transfer ideas – along with the rumours – around a business (we, as managers, should not forget that the reason rumours get such instant credence in business is that they are always more exciting and more interesting than the truth!).

While their lifestyle/workstyle needs are somewhat out of whack with the rest of the employees they constitute a powerful, if minority group. But as you struggle to build an engagement culture you should be aware of these people. Used effectively they can stand you in good stead. So, instead of dismissing them out of hand, perhaps in this new-age world we should be paying more attention to what they are capable of doing – for good or bad.

Every company, every division, every department has their Roger, Ricky or Rita as we shall call them. They are the people to whom others naturally go when they need information. Around the organisation, the Rogers, Rickys and Ritas know other Rogers, Rickys and Ritas – together they create an informal, highly effective network through which knowledge is easily transferred and – unbeknown to many – a significant amount of organisational learning takes place.

And it can be a real force for productive work. 'At one firm where I worked,' explains Swiss-based organisational consultant Patricia Seemann, 'we created a Yellow Pages directory that listed all the Rogers, Rickys and Ritas. We went around the company and asked where people went to get questions answered – in other words the selection was done by acclamation. Imagine my phone calls the day the directory was published and all the bosses found that they weren't listed? The reason was that no-one felt comfortable asking division heads and the like, and felt their knowledge was inaccessible.'

The Rogers, Rickys and Ritas are people with sharply honed social skills – they move and are accepted everywhere. The downside, of course, is that their influence can be a huge negative if they are not handled correctly. If you want to change the firm you need to get their buy-in early on. Otherwise they know best (and people accept that they know best) and are perfectly positioned (no matter how far down the corporate hierarchy they may be) to block any change they consider to be any kind of threat.

Patricia Seemann adds, 'If you lay-off any of the Rogers, a lot of the knowledge of the firm gets chopped off. The problem, of course, is how do you measure a Roger's work – it doesn't have tangible deliverables or expected output?'

Many managers regard Rogers as a menace (standing around the water cooler gossiping all day, which of course they also do). But, it may well be that it is on these informal networks (which have always existed and always will) that the people in our organisations may make sense of what is happening to them and help to meet the needs of their lifestyle/workstyle balance within the company.

If this is true, then these people have an ongoing critical role to pay and are indeed a critical resource in any business – especially in those where change is the constant.

New jobs for a new corporate age

How we need to think anew about engaging our mistrustful employees is one thing, getting a handle on what these people will be doing in terms of jobs is quite another.

There is a lot of evidence out there right now that points to some type of revolution in how our organisations will function in the future and how they will be staffed. Most of this is not predicated on it being a 'nice thing to do', but on the simple fact that our highly complex, technologically advanced and global businesses will demand it. While I don't predict the wholesale removal of marketing, finance, HR and other long-term job functions, we do see major change on the horizon, driven by necessity not fashion.

Business has changed so much in recent times that there are new imperatives driving our firms. These imperatives demand that we create new positions of responsibility and authority that have not existed before. Although not sure what their titles will be or just how wide their responsibilities, it is certain that we are on the verge of a new organisational structure that will require totally new jobs to achieve its goals. Indeed, what it most looks like is that job titles are going to be a wide, eclectic mix dependent on corporate culture, industry and the relative importance of the role.

Here are some of the new jobs that the twenty-first century business is going to need, and why we will need them.[2]

Corporate integrationists

These professionals are already a hot-ticket item for many corporations. Why? Well there are not many truly professional, skilled integrationists around and they are in very short supply. Why do companies need them? Following the acquisition craze of the 1990s many businesses never entirely got to grips with their new prizes. In case after case, they never actually got around to fully integrating the companies they had bought into one homogeneous whole. Now, they have an urgent need to make cost savings and 'manage the hell' out of their total operation. In doing this the skills of a corporate integrationist are paramount. They are able to look across management disciplines to see how the overall business could look by massaging all the parts in the right way. While a lot of this is based on getting the right sort of people equations in place and knocking down the silos of stand-alone corporate inefficiency, it is also about helping others in the business leverage savings and opportunities (eg better logistics, brand development, R&D sharing, bulk purchasing and so on). Whether they are called corporate integrationists or not, senior managers with these skills are deeply involved in redrawing the future of a host of corporations around the globe. Expect them to stay premium priced and in ever shorter supply. And a final word. If you find them, have a plan to retain them. These are the type of skills that are in such short supply that they are highly prized targets for almost any company and they are easily industry transferable.

Great salespeople

You could argue that great salespeople are always at a premium. But today this is different. Mostly because of the complexity of today's business operations, industry now needs a much smarter individual to lead the sales effort. Contracts are more complex – and often involve the bundling of several firms' services into one offer – last longer and often involve a board-level decision. To make these major sales, companies need highly sophisticated salespeople who not only understand the products or services and how they can integrate with others to make a compelling opportunity, but the ability to sell that concept at board level. These people have to be able to negotiate with senior management, but also have well honed people skills to lead and enthuse diverse teams of specialists. Already there is evidence that these people are in short supply.

Logistic gurus

There is no doubt that logistics (and that includes purchasing) is going to have a long-lasting influence on our businesses. Highly experienced logistics professionals are already in great demand, even to the extent of regularly crossing industry boundaries. The simple reason for their popularity is that they can make the difference between profit and loss throughout a business. Logistics in one form or another, is going to be one of the key drivers of the next economic cycle. Whether it is organising global purchasing opportunities, or delivering just-in-time solutions for manufacturing or customers, the logistics professional will become a major part of any corporation that makes, moves and markets stuff. And as manufacturing gets moved away to second- and third-tier suppliers, their role will become ever more important. Equally, in professional service firms, the logistics role is critical. One company calls its senior logistics professional the 'beach-master', echoing the role of the logistics chief in the D-Day landings who made sure that the front line forces were constantly supplied with what they needed to do the job.

Within the logistics boundary are other key players. Number one is the outsourcer. Outsourcing has now become one of the main tasks of industries that used to manufacture everything themselves. But as we know, outsourcing now covers everything from security and office cleaning, to manufacture, distribution, marketing, HR and after-sales service. Many managers believe that you can outsource anything if the price is right. There is little doubt that outsourcing is getting more and more prevalent. Not only that, it is finally being recognised as a job function in its own right. If you consider that up until recently, out-sourcing has been done by managers in different departments with no links to one another (HR outsources pensions and salary administra-tion; manufacturing outsources whole lines of products; IT outsources the entire management information system), then you can visualise what would happen if your Chief Outsourcing executive began to put a lot of this together. Outsourcing professionals are going to be key. They may carry a logistics title, they may even be those integrationists referred to above, but, whatever the job title, they will begin to revo-lutionise how we operate our businesses.

Multi-tasking general managers

The first thing to say about these people is that they are not a new talent discovery at all, they have always been there. It is just that no one has looked very closely at them for some time. Now they are back in fashion. Why? Consider this. You are opening an operation in China. What do you do, send a newly minted MBA? Of course not. What you need is a seasoned management professional who knows enough about your business, your products, people, finance and manufacturing to get the job done: the sort of person who hits the ground running and just keeps on running without calling head office all the time. Well, the good news is that they are still out there. The bad news is that a lot of them are needed as we expand our businesses so they are also going to be in short supply. Part of the reason for the shortage – as I explained earlier in the book – is that by the end of the 1990s we had a total fix-ation with narrower and narrower areas of specialisation. It was the era of the niche player. Unfortunately, we failed to give these niche players much in the way of general management, across-the-organisation skills. Now we are reaping what we so mistakenly sowed. If it wasn't so tragic, it would be rather amusing to realise that all this coaching and mentoring – sold to employees as a 'we really care about your development' story, is a belated attempt to pack some people skills into narrow, niche expertise, managers.

Senior-level people developers

Coaching and mentoring may be popular right now (for whatever reasons), but I am not referring to those. I am talking about the ravenous need by corporations to make their best people better. Take your top 10 per cent and make them 10 per cent more productive and you have a winning concept on your hands; at least that is the prevailing view of the majority. Several senior managers I discussed this with explained, 'It doesn't matter about the other 90 per cent, they'll do their jobs one way or another, *but* if we can get that top 10 per cent of our people doing 5, 10 or 20 per cent better, then we are breaking through all sorts of barriers and boundaries.' To do that corporations are going to need a whole new breed of development specialists who understand how to make the already exceptional even more so. Companies are already bringing these people on board (some firms use outside help, others claim that the confidentiality aspects preclude that) and they are tasked with one simple goal: 'Get the people we have identified as tomorrow's key players into the best shape you can.' Look for this 'crusade-to-be-better' to continue. And one final comment. Good coaches are very hard to find. If you find one, or two or three, do 'off limits' or 'exclusive' deals and tie them down.

Security hotshots

Post 9/11, corporations the world over went hunting for talent that could ring-fence their business. Now they have wised up a little and stopped pounding the panic button. That means that they have taken a measured, sober look at their needs, equating the search for the right talent to where they operate (geographically) and how their organisation functions. With that settled, most companies have concluded that they don't need Rambo-style lookalikes who can physically defend them. The real threat comes much more from computer-related crimes, most of which (due to deep corporate embarrassment) never get reported. However, all the organisations we have talked to have in one way or another accepted that an external hacker (even those just bent on simple-minded mischief) could seriously damage their operations. So security takes on a bigger role in these new business models as well.

Talent managers

Talent managers (or whatever you choose to call them in your business) are going to feature large in the business world of tomorrow, for the simple reason that we will not be able to sate our appetite for good people. Smart corporations have already done their homework, done their audits and know two things: (1) who they want to keep whatever the cost; (2) who they want to buy when they become available or go job hunting. We will all need talent managers in one form or another, be they former HR professionals or totally new recruits into the business world. Expect the best to be – as usual – in short supply.

Communication professionals

Communications, both internal and external, are set to take on a bigger and more overt role in all of our businesses. To make that happen we are going to have to find, train and develop a whole new set of professional skills (because there aren't many around right now), to lead revamped, and hopefully refunded, communication structures. Expect to see this as a new, exciting career path (that can well include responsibilities for shareholder relations and corporate social responsibility). Right now – like talent managers – there are not many of these professionals around, but expect the ranks to grow as firms rush to be more transparent and more accountable, motivated by the view that it's just good for business to do it that way. Chapter 6 explains further the role of the communication professional in the business of tomorrow.

There may well be other 'new jobs' in the business world of tomorrow. A case, for example, could certainly be met for a revised *HR manager*, one who will willingly lock horns with the CEO, and also gets his respect and full attention when people issues arise. The role of HR in developing employee respect and commitment is detailed in Chapter 7 later in the book, so the only thing to say here is that HR professionals are already taking on a different profile in many companies, and that certainly looks set to continue.

KEY ISSUES

- Prospective employees will 'audit' your business to check if it suits their lifestyle/workstyle.
- Having a 'real fit' between employer and employee will be of key concern.
- 'Will it enhance my career long term?' is the most important question of today's job seeker.
- Mobility expectations can turn off some people – don't make it a condition of employment.
- Take on the risk and move people up – or see them move out.
- Realise that you need to be open to recruiting a more diverse set of employees to attract the best talent available.
- Leaders need to be able to understand, empathise and manage employees with their constantly shifting lifestyle/workstyle patterns.
- In the new-age corporation are new-age jobs and responsibilities that will change the business landscape forever.

Notes

1 I am grateful to the UBS Leadership Institute and the FutureWork Forum for their valuable assistance in developing the criteria for engagement.

2 This listing has been updated and adapted from the original research published in JOHNSON, MIKE (2003) *Creating Dynamic Organisations: Human Capital Issues and Options for Tomorrow's Business.* Financial Times/Prentice Hall.

Chapter 6

Communicate!, Communicate!, Communicate!

The worse the news, the more effort should go into communicating it.

Andy Grove, chairman, Intel

What we've got here is a failure to communicate.
actor Strother Martin in the film *Cool Hand Luke*

Many years ago – 1977 to be precise – a book titled *Communicate*[1] was published. It may be three decades old, but I think that book still makes a whole lot of sense, and not just because I had a role in its creation. It was possibly one of the first truly to advocate the role of communications in an organisation and to stress how important it was to get this right, especially if you expected to recruit and retain the right people. The sad part is that in those 30 years, communication – and more specifically internal communication – has not moved along very much. It is still one of the poor relations of the organisational functions in the vast majority of companies, often under-funded and poorly staffed (in many SMEs it isn't really staffed at all). But if people are the critical resource and the key to our success, surely internal communications should be one of the most important support areas in any business?

In today's world, there are three major problems with internal communications:

- No one seems sure who should be responsible for it.
- No one seems sure of the skills required to manage it.
- No one is quite sure what it is supposed to be achieving.

After observing the efforts of hundreds of firms trying to organise internal communications, I have come to the conclusion that it doesn't really matter that much where it rests inside a business provided it receives sufficient profile to be effective. Often that is where things go badly wrong. It is parked – uncomfortably – in the wrong place for all the wrong reasons. There is nothing necessarily wrong with it being in, say, the marketing department of an organisation, as long as someone actually carries out internal communications. But if the whole focus, and budget and skills of the people are on external issues, then it just doesn't belong there.

I know of one major corporation, whose marketing efforts are centred almost exclusively around Formula One auto racing, who think internal communications – for which they are also responsible – begins and end with showing their race car to the staff. In reality, this means that there is no one to champion internal communications.

Sadly, this state of affairs tends to be all too prevalent. Internal communications is parked somewhere in the organisation, because no one quite knows what to do with it. And because it usually has pretty low-level people staffing it it never develops a voice of its own. As an old colleague of mind once said only half in jest, 'no one ever made vice-president or partner, by having responsibility for internal communications.' But that is a damning statement too. Because if we are to pay more than just lip service to the idea that our lifestyle/workstyle aspirants want open, honest, intelligent communication, then surely internal communications has a major role to play in keeping people informed and consequently engaged.

No one seems sure whose responsibility internal communications is

A study by the CIPD in 2003,[2] noted that 36 per cent of HR managers said they had lead responsibility for internal communications, compared to 41 per cent who reported that they shared the responsibility jointly with another department. This, of course is part of the problem: no one is quite sure where it belongs, it doesn't have a genuine corporate champion.

Having said that, there are firms – large successful ones at that – where the CEO sees himself or herself as the CCO (chief communications officer) and believes that his/her role is to inform staff personally of issues that affect them.

My view is that it probably doesn't matter where internal communications is located provided it has a senior management champion and is allowed to do its job. When you consider the complexity of the modern corporation, and the difficulty we all admit to having in getting messages understood by an ever more diverse workforce, then effective corporate communications become paramount.

Sadly, it would seem, resources for internal communications are set at either feast or famine levels. CEOs who see the real need to let employees know what is going on – this is very often in times of major change – will pour people and pounds into internal communications. A new arrival, particularly if times are reasonably stable, will be quite likely to de-emphasise internal communications, cutting both budgets and staff. In this respect internal communications seem to be set upon a permanent roller-coaster ride, boom to bust and back again.

If I were to locate internal communications anywhere it would be with HR, with a close relationship to external communications functions as well. Then I would have a senior executive at managing board level put in overall charge as part of his or her responsibility. It is vital to have a seasoned professional in this role who can act as a spokesman for the internal communications' group and enjoy ready access to the CEO.

The other point to keep in mind is that, like all other parts of an organisation, internal communications is not a role that is set in stone. There may be an imperative to build engagement, or there may be a need to help along a change process (perhaps associated with a merger or acquisition). Every so often, new issues will arise and need to be emphasised for a period of time. This is why you need a senior manager responsible who knows what is required. Too often the internal communications department just keeps cranking out the same old stuff, regardless of the real needs of the business at a particular time.

No one seems sure of the skills required to manage internal communications

I believe that you don't have to have a professional communicator as the head of internal communications. But you do need someone who can 'feel' what is happening in the business and knows enough to get things moving, briefing the professional communicators to do their job. My view – and one that has gained considerable credence in recent years – is that internal communications needs to be staffed by line managers (who may be on assignments from their other roles for upwards of 12 months). There is no reason why

you don't have to have a professional communicator as the head of internal communications. But you do need someone who can 'feel' what is happening in the business

marketing, manufacturing, legal or finance people cannot play a role in this catch-all position. They will bring a sense of the 'real world' with them and in turn will expand their own understanding of the organisation.

Too often, and here top management can take at least some of the blame, it is assumed that people in communications need to be able to write. No they don't! They need to have access to people who can, but they themselves need to know about the content of messages and understand the workings of the organisation well enough to hear the beat-on-the-street and how to respond to it. They need to be able to kick down the CEO's door and say 'Fred, we have to do something about this – quick.' Twenty-five-year-olds fresh from college or making coffee in the marketing department are not going to cut it. You need a seasoned professional who can 'smell' trouble. Supporting them you can have all the writers and marketing communications you want, either internal or external, depending on your budget.

My view – but I am biased, because I have spent 20 plus years making my living at it – is that it pays to go outside and hire horses for courses. For example: your vice-president of marketing is going to speak to a global marketing conference. Get a writer who can place your vice-president's message into the context of the world that those marketing executives inhabit. Similarly, if your CEO is going to speak at the Davos Symposium, get a writer who can put his comments into the context of the economic and political issues of the day. If your head of information systems is going to a technical conference in Palm Springs, get a writer who is steeped in tech lore (don't call me on this one, please!). Twenty years ago, all the big corporations had teams of writers on staff. Now, mostly, they have none. They go and find a writer who fits the bill. Also – as I have discovered – getting old and a little grey is great. I can go to a CEO and tell him honestly that I think his idea for a speech is a lousy one. Twenty years ago, I couldn't get away with it, I had to grow a moustache to make myself look older and more serious!

The rotating communication co-ordinator

One of the most successful internal communication operations in which I have been involved was at French Group Alstom – thankfully well before they nose-dived off the financial cliffs. There, internal communications did report to HR, who had inherited it along with a ragbag of other 'lost' departments in the course of a frantic three years of acquisitions. All the internal communications people reported directly to a plant manager as well, so there was conflict of loyalty. Worse still, in some of the acquisitions, strong-willed managers maintained a barrier against too much communication, hoping that the headquarters and its battalions of French *cadres* would eventually go away.

Of course they had no plans to do that. But, the first issue that had to be faced was communicating with the communicators. And there wasn't – as is so usual when it comes to corporate communications – much of a budget to effect change either. Anyway, working with the director of HR, I and several colleagues created a totally 'new-look' communications department. Key to our brief was getting everyone in the department thinking in the same way and sharing the same information and ideas.

First we carried out an audit on the people. We quickly discovered that while some had professional communications skills, others had just been saddled with the job, because no one else wanted it. However, through the audit we were able to establish who had what skills and how best they could be applied across the group.

Then – by collecting as much hardcopy evidence as we could from subsidiaries around the globe – we began to establish what sort of messages and signals were being sent to employees. To our shock, we discovered that these – until now – highly autonomous little communication units were pushing out all sorts of materials, very little of which had any connection with the corporate line being voiced from Paris.

We then unveiled our masterstroke. We established a group co-ordinator of internal communications at the Paris headquarters, *but* we made it a rotating job. And – thanks to the power of technology – also made it possible to do the job from virtually any location. So we picked, by universal acclaim, the first three people, who would each do the job for a six-month period. This worked extremely well and people became both very enthusiastic and began to share ideas with each other. The role of the co-ordinator was to help senior management develop the messages and then – using the skills inherent in the network – to get messages to employees. The additional bonus was that these co-ordinators quickly gained a true feel for the overall business, which they were able to take back to their units when their tour of duty expired. In addition, we created champions for the individual issues or technical aspects we were dealing with, allowing for an increase in pooled publishing and the like.

Each time the co-ordinator changed we had a group meeting to discuss and update each other face-to-face, hand out special assignments and form teams from different locations to work on specific issues.

No one is quite sure what is supposed to be achieved

First, you just have to keep it simple. Too many initiatives at once not only confuse people but make it impossible to track and measure success. I always advocate maintaining day-to-day information processes and then picking one or two big projects for each year to add some sparkle to the process.

> I always advocate maintaining day-to-day information processes and then picking one or two big projects for each year to add some sparkle to the process

At Alstom, being very specific, setting two or three main programmes, and using teams made up of communication professionals from around the group, we quickly built a pooled form of co-ordination, which became a very powerful weapon in pushing out across the globe the top management message of all working as one. So we knew exactly what we were trying to achieve – collectively – and how we would go about it. The simple point is, if you want to change people, make sure you change the messengers first. If they accept and sign up for the change you have won at least half the battle. Of course we still faced stubborn groups of hostile, 'dinosaur,' plant managers who didn't want to see a Paris-driven message in their factory. But with all the internal communications employees 'on message' it wasn't long before that petered out.

This method is both simple and cost-effective and modern technology means that it can be set up and operated for very little funding. The only additional cost was travel to meetings, but that was largely off-set by the savings made by pooling skills and resources. This, in fact, was probably the best part, and I would urge anyone else faced with creating a group internal communications process to do as we did. Once you know who can do what (and you'll be surprised how much hidden expertise you will discover) write it down and catalogue it and make sure everyone has access to this information on their intranet. Then keep it updated as new skills come on to the market. Everything was sent from the units to the co-ordinator, who then edited input and ideas and distributed it to the units, creating a constant two-way flow. They also 'policed' materials for quality and adherence to brand and design guidelines.

What we had done by the end – when it was running smoothly – was take a group of unhappy, cut-off, poorly trained employees and turned them into a multi-talented, multinational team with real curiosity and flair. They became powerful advocates and ambassadors of the change process we were trying to implement.

The 12 Cs of communication

I don't know if there are more of these, but since it is kind of fun, I'm going to stick with 12. I used to have only 11, but I've added number 12, not to make a nice round dozen, but because this last one ('common') is all about simplicity, basics. A basic premiss of internal communication is to strive to keep things simple. Too many people in this area try to complicate things. Guard against this. Pare down the message and keep it very, very straightforward. Watch the consultants you use and make sure that they keep it simple too. They'll want to make it really complex, because there's more work and therefore more money that way. Don't be tempted, keep it very simple indeed.

- Clear
- Concise
- Consistent
- Constant
- Candid
- Conspicuous
- Credible

- Categorised
- Current
- Cheerful
- Chatty
- Common.

Do these well and with enthusiasm and you could even be forgiven for a lack of professionalism! By that I mean that in so many cases there isn't a professional communicator (whatever that may be!) around. There's no PR agency or person from the communications department to help. You, Mr and Ms Manager are on your own. How do you get that all-important message across; how do you convey the notion that 'Hey, we are working in a pretty good place, let's stay a while.' If you want to appeal to those new-age life/work people we keep referring to, you can't do better than keep it simple, open and honest. That's the way to win hearts and minds. Even the shareholders like it simple.

Clear

Start from the questions 'What do I want people to understand?'; 'What should they take away from this communication?' Too many employee communications are too long, too complex and too, too boring. If you are not a professional (and if there aren't any available), write it in a narrative form. Think: 'How would I say this to people, what words would I use if I was in a face-to-face conversation?'

- Keep it clear.

Concise

For goodness sake keep it short. Most people's attention spans are tiny. If you want to get the message across, grab their attention and then get out.

- Keep it clear, keep it short.

Consistent

Remember what you said before. Maintain a link between your last communication and the next. Above all, don't get caught out with new messages wrapped up in 'sugar-coated' pills. It doesn't work and it insults the intelligence of people.

- Keep it clear, keep it short, keep it the same.

Constant

Don't stop – ever. Keep the news in front of people. Keep your hopes and dreams, successes and failures right up there. People don't respond to the occasional communication; it makes for suspicion. 'They only tell us something when they want something,' is a view I hear a lot. Smart communicators lay it on the line, all the time. Not too much, but whenever there's a good reason. And most times there is.

- Keep it clear, keep it short, keep it the same, keep going.

Candid

Above all, be honest. If you don't tell the truth your employees – plus the rest of the world – will find you out. We live in a world where any attempt to hide information is useless. Not only are your best employees well informed and intelligent, but most of the rest are too. Don't insult people, tell them the truth in a timely fashion. Above all don't try and influence or massage the message – employees will see right through you.

- Keep it clear, keep it short, keep it the same, keep it going, keep it honest.

Conspicuous

Make sure that what you want to tell them gets noticed and gets read. Don't try and be subtle. People get too many messages each day to want to read only yours. Your job is to get that communication in front of your employees and understood, any way you can.

- Keep it clear, keep it short, keep it the same, keep it going, keep it honest, keep it visible.

Credible

In addition to being honest, be credible. Employees know that if it's too good to be true it probably is!

- Keep it clear, keep it short, keep it the same, keep it going, keep it honest, keep it visible, keep it credible

Categorise it

Don't try and sell the same story to everyone – it doesn't work. Sell the same message, but don't tell the story the same way. Give the people at different levels the story in a way they want to read, that they can absorb, that means something to them, that is acceptable to them. Categorise your message to the groups that you need to explain the story to.

- Keep it clear, keep it short, keep it the same, keep it going, keep it honest, keep it visible, keep it credible and keep it categorised.

Current

Never, ever, wait to tell the story. These days immediate action is called for. Here's a tip: if for all sorts of reasons (legal issues spring to mind) you can't tell everything, tell something. If there is a communications vacuum it always gets filled with gossip and speculation. Why? Because rumours are always more interesting than the truth.

- Keep it clear, keep it short, keep it the same, keep it going, keep it honest, keep it visible, keep it credible, keep it categorised, keep it current.

Cheerful

Not an exciting word, cheerful, but it works for this stuff. Stay positive, keep it as light as possible, don't turn your message into some Wagnerian opus. Just keep it COOL. Don't listen to the doomsayers and the control freaks, keep it on message but with the slant firmly focused on the upside.

- Keep it clear, keep it short, keep it the same, keep going, keep it honest, keep it visible, keep it credible, keep it categorised, keep it current, keep it COOL!

Chatty

When in doubt about how to say something, just write it down as you would speak it. I know a lot of people who use pocket recorders to great effect. Just use your own words. Many of us don't have instant access to communication professionals in our day-to-day work, so think about what would make sense to you. Think of the messages you respond to.

- Keep it clear, keep it short, keep it the same, keep it going, keep it honest, keep it visible, keep it credible, keep it categorised, keep it current, keep it COOL and keep it chatty.

Common

Not a positive word, but by common I mean keep a common touch, don't use fancy words, don't try and appear superior. Think basic, short words and phrases, don't be pompous and don't have long paragraphs and obscure words or phrases. You'll get no brownie points for being clever.

- Keep it clear, keep it short, keep it the same, keep it going, keep it honest, keep it visible, keep it credible, keep it categorised, keep it current, keep it COOL, keep it chatty and keep it common.

if you follow these basic rules of communication you'll at least get the message across. Then of course there is the other small problem. Do they really believe it?

I guarantee that if you follow these basic rules of communication you'll at least get the message across. Then of course there is the other small problem. Do they really believe it? But, of course, even that isn't enough. Even if they read it, and even if they believe it, will they act upon it, will it lead to a modification in their behaviour?

The nine stages of a message

After the 12 Cs of communication, we have the nine stages of the message. 'Nine stages!' exclaim most people when you tell them this for the first time. But there are, and our memo to staff, our announcement of organisational change, must run through them all if it is to be in any way successful. I mean there is not much point in crafting and sending it in the first place if it isn't going to lead to some action or understanding is there?

A message must be:

1 sent
2 received
3 understood
4 believed or trusted
5 believed to be important to the organisation
6 felt (more than just believed) to be relevant to the employee personally
7 held at the front of the mind and acted on continuously (corporate values and goals)

8 'stored', then retrieved and acted on when necessary (operational information)

9 communicated to teams, customers and other external contacts.[3]

You can be pretty sure your message is being sent, has got off the blocks – but do you really know that it is completing the race? And if you do know that it is still in the race after hurdle five – 'message believed to be important' – (most messages crash out at this point), what can you do to ensure that it clears hurdles six to nine?

If your messages are not making it, here's a handy troubleshooter guide. The reasons can include the following.

- Key managers attend the global briefings, cascade meetings and so on. Although they may learn and absorb, they go home and carry on as before.
- Junior managers and employees complain that they do not know enough about corporate values, goals or strategies to do their jobs well.
- The intranet and other innovations are admired and then left unused or so overused that messages become redundant.
- Printed communications are read, believed, thought to be useful and then forgotten.
- Messages that are 'not relevant now' are lost forever.
- You are surprised and frustrated at how long it takes to get any real response to your initiatives.
- There are just too many messages out there. In the flow of 'chaff' people eventually give up reading anything at all.

Yes, corporate internal communications is fraught with frustration and hamstrung with hopelessness.

And certainly, the most worrying thing is the tendency to information overload. That is why it is very important to centralise the key messages. Sure you can deliver them in different ways in different places to make them understandable and palatable to a local audience, but you need to keep a hold on 'the message' at corporate centre.

Some years ago, I was involved with a major multinational that had expanded hugely through aggressive acquisition tactics. Their concern was that many of the key players in the companies they had acquired weren't playing for the new big team. Remember, it is always easier for communications when growth is organic, as you maintain your own people constantly. What the company in question did was set up two programmes.

Programme 1 was aimed at getting the top 250 people to understand that there was no going back and there was a single global company.

Programme 2 was aimed at getting the rank and file to understand the same message.

The tough part was programme 2. I was involved in auditing the messages that were circulating from formerly independent factories to the workers. The entire exercise was a nightmare. However, eventually, we managed to lay our hands on all the hard copy items: employee handbooks, newsletters, magazines, training videos and staff memoranda. We had them in every conceivable language (the company had been on a buying spree from Brazil to Bangladesh, from Spain to Sweden via the US and Canada). What we found was a huge shock. After sifting through this mound of communication material we realised that there were more than 80 (yes, 80) messages out there about what this company stood for and where it was going. And not one of them was correct!

We got hold of a big classroom in the corporate training and development centre and we covered the walls in everything from Polish newsletters to Portuguese handbooks. There were 23 versions of the company logo; seven different colours for the company logo and some give-away t-shirts from India with the wrong spelling. We brought the top 20 managers in to see our exhibition and they could not believe it. But it worked. We got their attention.

We then created an employee roadshow where, over a total period of three months, the four most senior managers (well at least the four who sounded credible and could present) divided up the globe and went to meet *every* employee (there were over 80,000). Every employee met them. Some were small groups, the Poles hired a soccer pitch), but everyone was able to ask a question if they wanted. We had a video and a text in local languages that described the organisation and its future and where they fitted into it all. Even the usually intransigent unions got involved and helped at local sites, sometimes acting as interpreters and organisers.

The message was uncompromisingly simple:

- This is who we are.
- This is where we (and therefore you) fit into the world economy.

- This is where we are going.
- This is what it means for your future.

At some locations (and I wish I had thought of this from the beginning) wives and children came to. We had a barbecue on a Friday night outside Barcelona for 1,600 people.

And the amazing thing about it all was that it wasn't that expensive to stage. We had our film costs, but the top four managers appeared in it and did the voiceover and we stole the rest of the film from the marketing department's product movies and spliced it together. Local country managers and division chiefs *had* to put local costs on their budget. For the corporate centre it was the cost of transporting four executives, and two technicians to each location. So you do South America in a week (and you do other stuff while you are there). Then you do North America, while someone else is doing Asia/Pacific and another is in Europe and the Middle East. Within four weeks – it took eight weeks to plan and get the hardware ready and translated into 20 plus languages – every employee had heard the exact, same message from one of the company's leaders. And it was simple. 'We have created this company because together we are not just stronger, but more agile, more productive and able to do things that we cannot do as small independent companies. We are here to secure your futures, your lives. Here is our order book, here is what we are going to do next.' Fifteen minutes plus a Q&A and everyone went home with a book and a video.

That is the largest-scale operation in which I have ever taken part. Eighty thousand people in two weeks! Not a bad piece of communicating.

But there's an unfortunate dénouement to all this. Six months after our efforts a new CEO took over. Instead of building a cohesive whole, he was there in the role of cost-cutter. Factories were closed and sold up. Some of the acquisitions were sold off, meetings of the top 250 people (which were to have been held every six months) were cancelled. We never saw the 80,000 people again. And they never saw top management either. The new CEO hid in his ivory tower in Frankfurt. Sadly too, the business declined. The good, the bad and even the ugly voted with their feet and moved on. It had been a great communication challenge and it had worked. Unfortunately, in the real world, nothing lasts for very long.

This may well be a good time to talk about corporate reputation and what that means in the whole battle for respect and commitment from Mr and Mrs lifestyle/workstyle.

A landscape strewn with fallen idols

The corporate scandals of the last few years have not helped the reputation of private enterprise at all. While one can have a rather 'I told you so,' attitude about some of the aggressive start-ups like Enron, the shaming of much more venerable, household names has been more difficult to accept. But what they do illustrate is that our highly complex, global businesses are almost impossible to manage perfectly every day, 365 days a year. Hardly a day goes by without a media report of yet another organisation whose accounts in one region or another don't add up, or have been over or under reported. Whether this is brought about by pressures to perform and be profitable I don't know. What it does do is create an increasingly poor reputation for companies in general and some corporations in particular.

Reputations take decades to build and can be destroyed practically overnight. Does this mean that all the employees are bad? Of course it doesn't. But it does mean that prospective employees are asking a lot more questions at interviews than they did. And your current employees are demanding a lot more disclosure from top management as to the real state of the organisation. If we are unable to give straight answers to direct questions we are certainly not going to be in a position to recruit and retain the right kind of people for our businesses.

Headhunters tell me that it takes a whole lot more these days to get candidates to change jobs. They really want to know what is going on in a prospective new company and a failure to tell them means they just won't sign.

Returning to my key theme once again: smart people usually tend to be responsible people. They demand to know what the organisation they work for is doing in their name. Similarly with investors, customers and suppliers. If those employees are bringing themselves to work every day, they are bringing to your office or factory their concerns about everything from the environment to accounting standards and stock price manipulation. That life/work balance concept begins outside your firm, not inside. And so, for example, we need to appreciate that our employees are first off ecologists, concerned waste-recyclers, members of Greenpeace, Friends of the Earth and the World Wildlife Fund. Their career choices are – one way or another – governed by these lifestyle beliefs. So, increasingly, they want to know if your organisation pollutes, from where does it source its raw materials, to which governments do you sell and so on. And if you cannot answer they don't want to join you.

So the ability to communicate what your organisation stands for and what its ethics are is vital to building that long-term respect and commitment. As I said earlier, honest, open communication is going to win the day every time.

So where does HR fit into all of this? Is HR ready and able to play its part in our aim of capitalising on people who want to be themselves at work and want their life/work balance to be in harmony? And if not, what will HR need to do, and need to be, to make it work. Chapter 7 hopefully holds the secret.

KEY ISSUES

- There must be a new – and revised – focus on internal communications.
- It needs the attention of a top management champion.
- A requirement for different skills from those of the past.
- Companies need to subscribe to the 12 Cs of communication: clear, concise, consistent, constant, candid, conspicuous, credible, categorised, current, cheerful, chatty, common.
- Understanding the 'journey' of a message is vital to creating an effective internal communications plan
- It takes new skills to effectively reach employees who inhabit a world dominated by creating a viable life/work balance.

Notes

1 NORTHCOTE PARKINSON, C. and ROWE, NIGEL (1977) *Communicate: Parkinson's Law for Business Survival.* Prentice Hall.
2 (October 2003) *HR Survey: Where We Are, Where We're Heading.* London. CIPD.
3 Adapted from a concept by Nick Winkfield of Stakeholder Studies.

Chapter 7

Creating commitment: the HR challenge

Here are all kinds of employers wanting all sorts of servants, and all sorts of servants wanting all kinds of employers, and they never seem to come together.

Charles Dickens

The future role for HR is as a change agent – with broader, more business-focused skills.

(2003) HR Survey, CIPD

In an October 2003 HR Survey, the CIPD reported that, 'one-third of HR practitioners currently see their primary role as being strategic business partners. Rather more than one in four see themselves as change agents and slightly fewer (24%) as administrative experts.' The CIPD goes on to report that, 'In terms of their preferred roles, that is, the one they would like to focus on in the future, nearly three in five aspire to be business partners, while the proportion who see their role as being administrative experts in the longer term falls to just 4 per cent' (see Table 2 on p131).

Further reporting on the findings of the survey, the CIPD went on to say: 'Although 23 per cent of respondents see their current role as being a business 'player', acting as a coach, architect and facilitator, only 15 per cent see this as their preferred role, possibly,' they comment 'because it would take them too far from their HR moorings. Relatively few senior HR people see themselves primarily as an 'employee champion' and fewer still would wish to do so.' This,' the

Table 2
HR ROLES NOW AND IN THE FUTURE

Category	Current role	Would like to play
Strategic business partner	33%	56%
Change agent	28%	30%
Administrative expert	24%	4%
Player	23%	15%
Employee champion	12%	6%

Source: (2003) Survey of 1,188 HR managers. CIPD.

report goes on to explain, 'may be partly because the language sounds unfamiliar to UK ears, or because employee relations issues are dealt with at a lower level within the organisation.'

The problem with these survey findings is that HR managers always say that they want to be more strategic, but in the real world they are bogged down in the day-to-day administration and support of line managers. What they need is a concerted plan to break out. Outsource the administration if necessary (although that has a backlash all of its own if it isn't handled well) and move into that more strategic role.

Well maybe. My concern is the total lack of interest in being the 'employee champion,' because I think that is a major role for HR in the future. Not in sticking up for individual employees, but for all of them collectively. Someone needs the role of the conscience of the business and that is one – just one mind you – of the roles that HR needs to assume.

Someone needs the role of the conscience of the business and that is one – just one mind you – of the roles that HR needs to assume.

As I have already explained throughout this book, businesses today – regardless of size or industry – are complex, cruel places. If we are to employ all these people with their life-work needs and their expectations driven by lifestyle and workstyle, then we need an employees' champion. A person to take care of the people. That role has to be in HR. As psychologist Elisabeth Marx has explained to me on numerous occasions, 'CEOs are NOT people people at all.' In 99 per cent of cases she is right. They are far too busy cutting deals and worrying about quarterly results to worry about the people. No matter what their pronouncements about 'people being their greatest asset,' they need someone else to do the people-relations work. That, I think, means that HR gets the job. I mean, you are not going to make the finance director the people's champion are you?

And there are some very good reasons for having HR as the employees' champion. They are a natural support function, most HR people have a genuine empathy and they understand the need to keep people up and running, fuelled with knowledge and commitment. Not that they can't be hard-headed and business-like about this task. They *need* to be hard-headed. But they can form a terrific bridge between the top management strategists and the rank and file of the business.

Consider, if you will, the fact established earlier in this book, that the people we are employing intend to be themselves at work. Our Greenpeace activist, our weekend Hell's Angel, our sailor, swimmer and skier, all bring themselves and their personalities, traits and interests with them to work each day. If we want to engage them fully – while also understanding the personal aspects of their lives – we need to have a function within the business that can ensure that relationships between the firm and its employees work. A function that respects a person's lifestyle choices and in consequence earns that person's respect in return. I see that most clearly as a job for HR. Maybe not every HR person, but the majority need these skills of understanding employees' needs: and they need them *now*.

So, let's not get too enmeshed in this strategy debate. Let's do some good work on the engagement front first. The results that flow from having an engaged workforce will give you the credibility to help further your ambitions as a strategic business partner.

Later in this chapter, I am going to outline what I see as the array of responsibilities that HR has in the organisation of the future, but all of them are built around one premiss: being the 'engagement' head of the business. HR is the Pied Piper of the firm, gaining the employees' trust and commitment.

It is interesting to see in the conclusion of the CIPD 2003 survey the comment that, 'The boundaries of the HR function are becoming more diffuse as HR establishes strong links with other business functions. The scale of response in internal communications suggests that HR is competing effectively with the marketing function for the job of ensuring that messages are taken on board.' It ends by saying, 'As we are increasingly aware of the importance of trust in maintaining employee motivation and commitment, there are clearly opportunities for HR to strengthen its position in this area.'

But that employee motivation, commitment and respect don't come cheaply. What needs to happen quickly – as the CIPD survey suggests – is for HR to divest itself of non-core activity and take up the position of corporate engagement officer. Now that would look interesting on a business card!

However, there is plenty to keep the HR department busy. Based on interviews in Europe and the US with senior managers, here are just some of the items on HR's 'to-do' list:

- Aligning HR strategy with business strategy.
- Getting the succession planning and recruitment things right.
- Getting the outsourcing thing right.
- Getting the reward strategy right.
- Getting the assessment thing right.
- Getting the coaching thing right.
- Getting the golden handcuffs on star talent.
- Measure!, measure!, measure!
- Managing the boss.

Aligning HR strategy with business strategy

Sounds like a plan doesn't it? Trouble is, in a lot of companies HR has its plans and they don't dovetail with the strategic plan – well not much of it. Indeed, a study by the Industrial Relations Service (IRS) says that 'at first line level of management, where good HR is paramount, the majority of managers do not have goals aligned to HR strategy.' IRS' managing editor, Mark Crail commented, 'one of the most bizarre findings of the survey was that most firms had separate HR and organisational strategies, but bringing these together is a huge task and there is a practical limit on how long you can keep upsetting the work people do.' He added, 'Overall, the number of firms actively engaged with human capital management was very low. We have a long way to go.'

On the basis of that evidence, organisations most certainly have. But it is vital if we are to engage with these new-age employees that management (and that *must* include HR) aligns its plans and actions throughout the business. The danger here (and one of the permanent criticisms of a lot of HR activity) is that it isn't focused on the practical needs of the business. HR must support the business strategy with practical action. In this case action translates into ensuring top management understand the need to address these lifestyle employees in the right way, and setting up policies and procedures to recruit and retain them.

There simply cannot be an HR strategy that is different from that of the business strategy. It makes absolutely no sense at all. HR's role is as a supporting member of the organisational cast. Its job is to help other managers across the organisation understand the importance of developing skills and understanding of the life-work equation that is the bedrock of most employees' behaviours and beliefs. As the life-work champion, they have a duty to speak for the employees, to reveal clearly what the human resources of the business expect.

Getting the succession planning and recruitment things right

This is closely linked to the alignment of business and HR strategy. HR cannot fulfil its mission to support the other functions with the required human resources if it doesn't know which people are required. Therefore, it is vital that HR's people-procurement strategy is part of the overall business strategy. Senior managers I talked to in the last 12 months say that this is still an area where companies stall in their ability to perform effectively. 'In recession, no one worries about keeping the pipeline for new people pumping. Then things get better and we scramble to hire people again.' However, HR has a duty to know what the long-term strategy is in terms of future manpower requirements, so they can at least be ready to spring into action. Equally, within the firm, high potentials need to be identified ready for redeployment.

Getting the outsourcing thing right

If HR – or large parts of it – are to concentrate of the real, emerging people issues and are going to be dedicated to building an engagement culture, then they don't need to be involved with mounds of administrative detail. Having said that, a great deal of what HR can outsource cannot just be pushed out of the door and forgotten. It needs professional attention and management and someone on staff to ensure that things happen as they should. There is little point in outsourcing services, in order to free up time to devote to an employee engagement strategy, when your chosen outsourcer is destroying your employees' commitment through their actions. While I don't want to turn this into an outsourcing advice centre, I have detailed some advice on good practice in outsourcing in the box on p142,

Getting the reward strategy right

Today, reward is more than just salary and bonus, especially for the individuals who make up the vast majority of our knowledge workers. Personal and professional development are seen by our new-age lifestyle employee as a critical part of their reward package. Assessments (see below) to aid them in refocusing their personal and professional lives are also a key element of the reward process. Coaching and mentoring (again see below) are also part of the non-cash reward process. Additionally, as we have already mentioned in a previous chapter, time off, sabbaticals and the opportunity for new experiences are all up there with traditional perks. But again, this has to be offered on the individual level to meet each employee's unique expectations and demands, and with the understanding that these expectations and demands will change with time. With our employees living their continuously changing lifestyle, we who seek to employ them need to continue to assess those needs.

I think these 'time off' demands are going to be one of the most interesting to see companies deal with. Whenever I meet people to discuss perks this comes up, but it is the strangest phenomenon, coming as it does when there seems to be a huge trend to move jobs to other countries where labour costs less. It seems that the disconnects in our society are very much with us. The old managers – probably more used to a six-day, sixty-hour week than four days' work and three days off – just don't get this stuff. And yet I am hearing this from the new-age workers in the US, in the UK and right across Europe. As I said in the opening chapter, people seem to be trying to un-complicate their lives and find simpler ways of life-work balance. So when you come to assess rewards, think carefully about what constitutes a reward today. Knowledge workers in particular don't see nine to five as a way to fulfil their lives. They'll work for us, but they also want to 'play' and their play is very different from previous generations.

As to 'real' rewards, they are set to do two, seemingly opposite, things. Get simpler and more complex at the same time. What I mean by that is that most companies are looking to create common compensation platforms where – except for the impact of local taxation and possibly very weird cost-of-living hikes – everyone is rewarded in much the same fashion. That's the simple part. The other part is that everyone wants to be able to access what they want, when they want it, at a time that suits their lifestyle. We can readily outsource a lot of this, but we have to keep hold internally of the individual assessment process.

Finally, several of my work colleagues, who know a lot more about compensation than I do, have suggested that long-term compensation (that's the stuff that makes you long-term rich) is set to go underground. By that I mean that experts I talk to say that a company's long-term compensation programme for its top executives (say top 250 for example), will be viewed as a competitive advantage and senior managers will have to sign-up never to disclose how it works. It will do two things. Make top performers seriously rich and lock them into the organisation. But few people will get to know the ingredients. This is a very interesting idea, because as most companies cut final salary pensions and the like, it is likely to lead to an 'us' and 'them' compensation model. Fine if you are invited into the gilded cage yourself, of course.

Getting the assessment thing right

Assessment (together with the twins coaching and mentoring, of which more later) has been a 2004 management fad. The supposed need to assess people's needs is a great idea if it is done correctly. But although HR's responsibility, it is important to do some assessment before you begin the assessment, so to speak. If you are operating in a climate where there is fear and resentment, guard against making it worse. Assessment is intended as the first building block in creating training, development, coaching and mentoring plans. As such it needs careful handling.

One global company boldly introduced an assessment process that went badly wrong. Employees assumed the assessment process was a preparation for a major redundancy programme. Such was the level of demotivation and fear that the unions were called in and the company had to close the whole process down.

At others, where it has been introduced with the right level of pre-assessment communication and explanation, it has worked well. Companies are even using the process as part of the non-cash reward programme. By giving people in-depth assessment they are not only able to get a good picture of their professional development needs but have been able to extend it to cover their employees' personal lives as well. This plays particularly well with our new-age life-work balance group, who are very open to the idea of knowing your strengths, weaknesses and opportunities for further development in both business and private lives.

Assessment is the perfect example of how to engage positively with our lifestyle-driven employees. They *want* to know more about themselves and they

> Assessment is the perfect example of how to engage positively with our lifestyle-driven employees. They want to know more about themselves

want to be able to learn and grow and challenge themselves. Any organisation that isn't doing professional and personal assessment of its people as part of an ongoing programme is missing out on a huge opportunity to engage them more fully and thus earn their respect and commitment.

Getting the coaching (and mentoring) thing right

As I have already said, coaching (and mentoring) are not perks. If you want to engage with lifestyle-driven employees (and you don't have much choice) this is not an option but an intrinsic component of what they consider their reward package. As they would say, coaching rocks. They need and expect to improve, both in professional and in personal ways. Due to the recession, and consequent lack of finance, we have denied this benefit to employees for quite some time, so we had better get good at it providing it now. When I talk to people about this, I find that it is difficult to pin down any kind of norms in the way companies approach coaching and mentoring. Suffice to say, you must know, pretty well, what people expect in your business. Let them get the best that you can afford. Do it soon and you might just begin to halt the exodus of talent.

However, before you leap into the great coaching and mentoring action plan, there are some things to consider very carefully.

Check out the coaches

Who is going to be a coach? There are a lot of people around who are, frankly, just not good enough. Check out your coaches as you would any other employee or supplier. Where have they worked; who recommends them; what are their results?

And make sure the service is on *your* terms not theirs. Remember who is paying the bill here. It is for your employees you are doing this.

On the other hand, when you are hiring externally, please don't be too parsimonious – it isn't a good idea. If you try and negotiate fees downwards too much, you'll get a coach who either doesn't care enough or feels resentful. And it will manifest itself to the people he or she is there to work with.

Here's a negative for you: if you get it wrong the response will be 'They love us so much, they hired *this* guy to coach us?' Not the reaction you want – ever.

It is exactly the same with mentors. Although most of them are drawn from your own staff, you still need to know how good they are. A great mentoring relationship can really build huge opportunities inside organisations. And, as I said earlier, help everyone to learn a lot more about the business. The other thing it can do is free up ageing top managers – who may be blocking the way for others – to play a very real role in your business.

Getting the golden hand-cuffs on star talent

This isn't going to be an optional task either. HR will have to assume responsibility for developing new ways to lock in the talent you need to make the business succeed. Obviously, line managers and top managers will help in identifying and sourcing these people. But the creation and execution of programmes to chain-down business talent are going to be the responsibility of HR. Long-term incentives will obviously dominate, with those based on personal or organisational performance expected to be the strategy of choice. However, increasingly in world-class firms, rewarding HR professionals for their ability to 'hold' key players is increasing.

Measure !, Measure!, Measure!

Quantifying, measuring, having a real set of numbers to explain your achievements in HR are going to become common practice. Don't ever say, 'we're too small for this stuff.' You're not. At least not in the new-age economy. As HR consultants, Towers Perrin, explain, 'The HR function has been among the slowest to quantify its impact on an organisation, in part because much of its work relating to employee performance and engagement has been impossible to measure.' They add, 'While HR has long looked at things like turnover, headcount, recruitment costs and training costs, the notion of determining a true return on investment in people has remained elusive.'

Towers Perrin go on to suggest that, 'This is changing fast. Partly because of cost pressures and management's need to better understand the relative value of investments in various employee programmes.' And so emerging new tools, 'now allow employers to quantify the relationship between employee and customer behaviours and financial outcomes and drive behaviours in ways that lead directly to the right outcomes.'

Certainly in the future demographic and staffing models will help to identify the changing profiles of workforces. What I hope they also do, is begin to identify the changing lifestyle/workstyle needs and expectations of every individual you employ. Without that, you will never anticipate what is going to happen next. And CEOs do not like surprises!

Norman Walker, until recently the global head of HR at pharmaceutical giant Novartis, says that, 'Of course we need to be able to measure human resource outcomes. If HR processes aren't business processes, then we can never be able to really take part in the strategic debate.' He adds, 'Our biggest issue as professional HR people is to make sure that the technology can give us fact-based credibility.' He ends, 'Fact-based credibility is the language of business. Right now only finance has this, we need to have it too.'

Most definitely. Being able to put a price on everyone's head, in terms of wants, needs, expectations and how much they cost to employ; as well as how much they'll cost you if they leave, is the only way to go. If you cannot quantify the impact of your people, you won't be able to compete with the rest of the business.

Just a thought

A lot of these initiatives are not only difficult to kick-off, they are equally challenging to implement and sustain. Depending where you and your colleagues are in the corporate food chain, it could well pay to have a sponsor from top management lead the fight. My view – and the view of many savvy professionals – is, 'Don't try and go it alone', use a top management champion to make it work, and, if necessary, let them take the credit. You'll get your reward later in a smooth operating, recruitment, retention and reward system.

New rules – new job titles?

When David Bell left the *Financial Times* newspaper to become the HR director of its parent company Pearson, he insisted that his job title become Director for People. The finance director immediately retorted that in that case he should be called Director for Money, but there is something in a name. How about these:

- chief talent officer
- chief people developer/head coach
- chief life-work balance officer
- chief rewards executive
- chief of culture relations
- keeper of the corporate conscience.

Here's how some of these will work:

Chief talent officer

We will soon again be facing a talent famine and this role will be crucial to any business's attempts to sustain success. The chief talent officer is going to be charged with the responsibility for finding and holding the best talent you can get for the money. Not only that, with a premium on good people, one of the keys to this job will be to have enough 'helpers' to locate and sign-up good people before the competition. That means getting into bed with the very best in executive search and recruitment (because you won't be able to do it all internally). That means having permanent searches underway – globally – for top performers. It will also mean knowing the strategic direction the company is going in, in order to be able to provide the needed human capital at the right time. So, in addition to managing people IN, it will entail the professional managing of people OUT when they have completed assignments. It will also include working with a second level of 'contracted' staff, who may well work for other businesses. It is going to be a lot more complex than in the past.

Chief people developer/head coach

A lot of what HR-style people will do will focus on making the people you have already hired better than ever. They, of course, will expect life-long learning as part of the overall reward process. Additionally, senior

HR people will be expected to make sure that the top team is constantly up to speed and know where to access the very best in learning and personal development experiences.

Chief life-work balance officer

As we have seen throughout this book, life-work balance is not going to blow away, it is here to stay. How you harness it inside the business may vary, but those that recognise and celebrate flexibility and diversity will most probably have an edge on the competitors. Having formal programmes that meet, exceed and develop with people's expectations has got to be the way to go. You will have a more motivated, educated and productive workforce as a result.

Chief rewards executive

Reward programmes are going to be very different as people seek – and receive – a broader range of rewards based on their present circumstances. Again, the smart companies who allow employees to choose the package that fits their lifestyle will be winners.

More than that, we will begin tying managerial rewards down to whether or not we as managers can motivate our teams. And in case you don't see it that way, smart companies are already doing it.[1]

Two hundred and fifty HR managers were asked the question, 'In the future, do you think that at least part of the salaries and bonuses for executives and managers will be based on their ability to maintain a satisfied workforce or create a talented team?'

Yes, it is already happening	27%
It will happen soon	33%
It is something that will eventually happen	30%
I don't think so	6%
Not stated	4%

Chief of culture relations

We got a long way without mentioning culture. But a good or a bad culture in the company is going to be a crucial measurement device. If the culture is negative then you are going to have to spend a great deal of time trying to turn it around. Places with positive culture will become true talent magnets, where reputation alone will ensure a steady supply of the right people.

Keeper of the corporate conscience

It seems to me that it is HR, or whatever HR will metamorphose into, that will assume the mantle of keeping the conscience – the ethical flame – of the business alive. Corporations need to be able to look back at their history and it seems that HR-related skills are best suited for this.

The future: supermanagers?

So, far from being eliminated, industry experts see HR responsibilities as crossing the whole of the organisational spectrum. But it is going to be a very different type of role in order to fulfil all these functions. The thoughts of most commentators are leaning toward the idea that we will see a supermanager emerging: what one senior executive termed a 'transformer'. This person will help people work and develop and in the process have a stake in part of the ongoing transformation of the business. Because, in the view of those I talked to in my research, our businesses are not static bodies, but living entities in constant flux and development. We have to work with individual employees who are personally undergoing the same process of change. To manage these dynamic processes requires people with vision, but also people who value the human contribution above all else.

> The thoughts of most commentators are leaning toward the idea that we will see a supermanager emerging: what one senior executive termed a 'transformer'.

Best practice guidelines for outsourcing
These guidelines are adapted from the publication *Outsourcing in Brief*[2] which I wrote in 1997 in an attempt to explain what was then the emerging outsourcing phenomenon. Since then outsourcing has become a huge global business. But the basic management principles of how to get it right still apply.

Management issues
- Retain in-house control over strategic direction.
- Retain responsibility for setting standards to which the supplier must conform.
- Use a prime contractor.
- Make the supplier responsible for delivery.

- Be prescriptive about the service requirements rather than the method of service delivery.
- Never lose sight of the business-driven objectives of outsourcing.
- Avoid lock-in to any single supplier.
- Expect value-for-money, but accept the supplier's need to make a profit – a partnership.
- Understand the strategic, political and managerial implications of the scope of your outsourcing.
- Define the supplier's points of contact – ensure adherence.
- Have an appropriate person to manage the contract.
- Keep the procedures simple.
- Regularly review the outsourcing contract and relationship with the supplier.
- NEVER stop negotiating.
- Re-tender contracts at defined intervals.
- Regularly review the outsourcing market to identify trends and changes.
- Monitor supplier's resource levels and business knowledge.
- Encourage co-operative contract evolution and take advantage of developing technologies.
- Retain and exercise the right to conduct IS audits at the supplier's premises.
- Aim for continuous improvement.

HR-specific issues
- Ensure sufficient number and quality of in-house staff remain to manage the outsourced situation.
- Promote a continuing bond between supplier staff and end-users.
- Make the morale of supplier staff a customer concern.
- Sort out personality conflicts as soon as possible.
- Review regularly in-house staff skills and numbers.
- Involve end-users in monitoring service delivery against targets.
- Retain the right to veto supplier's choice of key staff.

Service/business issues
- Match expectations with needs, not historical achievements.
- Have a contingency escape plan covering the outsourcing contract, software ownership etc.
- Maintain the right to invite tenders for new work.
- Recognise that requirements will change and be willing to adjust costs accordingly.

- Ensure that service-level agreements are always realistic and do not expect them to remain static.
- Continue to benchmark the service and consider alternative approaches.
- Discuss with all concerned, at the earliest possible stage, plans which could affect services.

Communications/understanding issues
- Clearly define the scope and interface of what is outsourced.
- Establish unambiguous roles and responsibilities for the customer, end-user and supplier.
- Maintain regular customer/supplier contact at various levels – even when things are going well.
- Establish an open relationship, be prepared to compromise.
- Build a relationship of trust with the supplier.
- Hold regular meetings to monitor achievements.
- Define clear escalation procedures.
- Do not abuse escalation procedures – nit-picking with managers is counter-productive
- Encourage the supplier to propose changes based on their expertise.
- Ensure customer awareness, understanding and commitment.

Using or adapting this checklist, fleshing it out to meet you own specific needs, as well as sharing it with others can only contribute to the overall success of the HR outsourcing process.

KEY ISSUES
- HR, a supportive, strategic business partner.
- HR's 'to-do' list is changing its emphasis AND getting longer.
- HR must be able to measure its activity, otherwise it will never fully engage with top management.
- HR's responsibilities broaden to meet emerging corporate needs and issues, across a broad spectrum, from chief talent office to keeper of the corporate conscience.

Notes

1   Results of a poll of 250 HR managers at the October 2002 Richmond Events European HR Conference

2   MIKE JOHNSON (1997) *Outsourcing in Brief*. Butterworth Heinemann.

Chapter 8

What's going to happen next?

Some people will like me and some won't,
so I might as well be myself,
and then at least I'll know that the people who like
me, like me

Hugh Prather

On the evidence of what employees say, there is no doubt that our businesses are going to change dramatically over the next decade. And while we can be thankful that technology is coming to our rescue, I think we are going to have to do a whole lot more than simply rely on that. Because, unless we can not only manage, but also empathise with, our employees, we are not going to get very far.

Throughout the research for this book I have recorded two key facts:

- Employers (like you) want to be able to measure better, so that you can put monetary value on the HR function. You need, you tell me, to be 'more scientific', more 'like finance', more 'aware of the costs of employment.' Well that will get you a date with the CEO anytime.
- Employees (like yours) want to be left to their flexible lifestyle/workstyle choices. They don't want to be a cipher, a number, a statistic that you can read like a balance sheet. Indeed, their checks and balances are all about being real, being human.

How do we begin to reconcile these twin expectations: one corporate, one individualistic?

In some ways, it would seem that we are demanding that HR professionals become more scientific and spend more time measuring human performance than ever before. This at a time when individuals – including all us managers too – are deciding that we want to be, simply 'US.' And we want to be 'us' at work, 'us' at home – 'us' everywhere.

There is a huge dichotomy in this. Made worse by the fact that we have a serious shortage of real managers who can effectively 'do' the people thing. It almost seems a perfect example of poor planning. You want ever more scientific measures, the employees want to be left alone to do the job.

There are a few things, however, that will save us. First we are not really very good at measuring. Second it is doubtful that the majority of corporations will achieve this aim anytime soon.

Therefore what I suggest is that when you consider 'What happens next?' in your business, you take into account these stirrings in the real world and make some adjustments to your plans.

There is no reason why you cannot measure, but please be sure what you want to measure.

There is no reason why you cannot begin to manage these people, but please be sure you get some managers who can *manage* and don't just have the word in their job title.

A careful plan, a well-sold plan, followed up with real commitment, will pay dividends in the months and years to come. It is just going to seem a little odd to begin with. To help, at the end of this chapter, I'll give you some of the insights I have picked up about how to sell these ideas to the CEO and your fellow top managers. You probably have your own ideas, but maybe I have been able to distil some thoughts and actions from other managers, the few who have already recognised the trend toward life/work balance, that might help you.

But first, let's look at what the future holds and how, by putting it into the new lifestyle context, you can begin to formulate the best ways, not only to manage, but also to build committed, productive employees.

Get some managers who can manage

In the future – and that starts now – we are going to have to place some fresh emphasis on people management and reward people for being good at it. There can't be any excuses any longer. So we will have to invest a great deal of time, effort and money in making managers and leaders out of specialists. The great corporations are already on their way with this, pouring millions of dollars, euros and pounds into it.

They already know that they have to be better, that it is not enough to hire and hold technical geniuses.

An example of that is in the banking industry, where they are dividing up the work so that the smart, technical people who are never going to be people managers, get to do their job, while a people manager makes sure all those specialists have their wants and needs fulfilled. The people manager's bonus depends on how the job is done, measured by the overall performance of the team he 'manages' and the retention rates. This sort of example is going to spread to other industries very quickly. The people manager is, in fact, a sort of junior talent manager – ever watchful for the emerging needs of individuals in his or her group and solving them. If we are in a tech-driven world, we can be sure that not everyone will want to be a people manager or that everyone will succeed in this role. The organisation

> The people manager is, in fact, a sort of junior talent manager – ever watchful for the emerging needs of individuals

outlined above seems a good option. But think back to what I explained earlier. We currently have well-meaning managers getting it wrong. Managing *their* way is not the way to meet individual employee expectations.

Hiring teams of talent

In 2004, hiring teams of talent has spread from its traditional home of the finance industry to a host of other areas. Merger and acquisition teams, legal teams, research teams, IT teams and groups of chemists have all been 'bought' en masse. In another move, companies have been acquiring smaller start-ups and specialist operations simply for the people working inside them (it is cheaper to buy the company than hire a headhunter to take them out one by one).

Hiring teams of talent is set to be big business in the future, so we all need to do a quick audit of our businesses and see if there are any teams on the danger list. If you don't know where you are vulnerable you can get a very big surprise one Monday morning when half your IT department doesn't show for work. As the economy ramps up and companies start casting their eyes around, things will get very exciting very quickly. During the course of writing this book I had a conversation with a senior executive in one of the world's leading IT outsourcing firms. He explained to me that in Europe alone in the next three years, there were upwards of 100 major new IT projects with a value of at least £500 million, and these projects would require up to 100,000 new people to staff them. Where are they coming from? Your organisation!

The talent agent finally arrives

The talent agent's arrival has been touted for years. Now they have arrived. Not too many at present but watch them develop. Their starting base has been in the interim management business. Interim management is now not just a respectable industry in which to be – it meets perfectly the lifestyle/workstyle wishes on the new-age employee. Why? It creates choice and freedom. There is always someone ready to employ talent, especially when you can send it back when you don't need it.

These employees are very flexible. Contracts rarely run beyond nine months, at which time they can choose to disengage for a time or leap back into the working world. Those currently running interim management firms – and they are increasing daily – are the new talent agents and they are meeting the needs of both sides and that's what makes good business. On one side, a company gets a qualified person with no need for training and who can be immediately effective and doesn't cost the earth to remove where their usefulness is over. On the other side, the interim executive gets flexibility and the opportunity to do the lifestyle things they want between assignments.

Expect a lot more employees to opt for this sort of working life in the years to come.

Share your talent with others

Every time I raise this issue, the sceptics are quick to pounce on it, usually saying that this could never happen in their organisation due to confidentiality issues and so on. Well, once again, those that refuse outright to consider new ways of working are going to lose out. And they are going to lose out even further as the lifestyle/workstyle revolution reaches maturity. If we are not able to use the services of excellent people on a part-time basis we may not get them at all. Equally – as with interim managers – we might not need them all the time either. And we as businesses will be involved with so many joint-ventures and alliances that it will become natural to share experts between ourselves.

Indeed, a lot of alliances and joint-ventures are already predicated on the grounds of the partners sharing access to each others' technologies, which really means the 'brains' that have built it.

So learn to share, because it is yet another factor in the new age.

Working with outsourced 'employees'

This trend has been building for some years and might have got a little side-tracked in the recession, but it is coming back fast. By outsourced employees, I mean those that you do not directly control. This area is set to grow quickly now that companies once again need more people. There is a mounting body of evidence that companies are not going to go on massive hiring sprees. Instead they will turn to professional people outsourcers, like Adecco and Manpower, to provide the required staff. What is important for your organisation here – apart from the need to ensure you get the all-important agreements with the out-sourcing firm correct (see box on p142) – is to make sure you have managers in place who can manage people who are not on your payroll. This calls for negotiation and persuasion skills and obviously good people management. Once again, the development of successful people managers becomes vital.

Hire and hold the oldies

Got a plan for the over-50s? You need one – *now*. We are going to run out of talent pretty quickly, so the over-50s who want to work may well be our saviour. However, as I have pointed out elsewhere in the book, treat them in the right way and use them for their talents – don't let them get in the way of new talent eager to move up.

Diversity rules

As with the over-50s, you need a dedicated plan to manage diversity. In the future we are going to need to manage a much more diverse work-force if we expect our businesses to grow. Some firms are very good at this: The Savoy hotel in London (with its business only in the UK) has 42 nationalities on its staff – a really eclectic mix. Others are not nearly so adventurous, but need to be to avoid starving themselves of talented individuals who might just want to spend some time in their business.

Get a diversity plan in place (to cover top management too!).

More of the action

This could be subtitled, 'Do the SME's win?' Well if we cannot make work interesting and get people engaged in it, the answer is 'Yes' they do. As for those bright people we all want to have in our businesses, survey after survey reports that they see small and medium enterprises as not only more interesting, but more caring about employees' wishes too. So they are, in reality, the perfect place for lifestyle, want-to-be-myself-at-work people to go. This means that we are going to have to be prepared – if we are not an SME – to begin to manage more as if we were. Those soulless corporations and public sector monoliths are going to have to get their communication and their leadership right to meet the needs and expectations of those who would rather be working in a cosier climate. And there is no real reason why that cannot be achieved. As I pointed out earlier, if banks can appoint people managers then so can others. Small, work-friendly units can make even the most gigantic organisation feel like a small enterprise. I see an ever-increasing role for HR in staffing these units (or having people managers who are part HR person and part specialist).

As we continually emphasise, organisations must have a corporate rethink as to how they are going to make people want to work for them, who are the people that can make that happen successfully and what kind of training they will need.

Time and again I hear of small business units in big businesses where people stay for years and years because they are happy with their colleagues and the scale of what they are asked to do. If we can get these people managers on board, empowered perhaps to make work-related decisions such as extra time off, job sharing, days working at home, etc we can create some very dynamic businesses that fulfil employee expectations.

The age of the unknown competitor

I used to ask the question, what do American Express, Federal Express and Manpower have in common? The answer is that around 50 per cent of all their people are interchangeable. IT and its derivative parts drive those businesses and make them successful in their ability to collect money or distribute goods or people fast. In the future we are going to have to look a lot harder to see where the competition lies and see who is sneaking up behind us.

Part of the reason for this is that jobs are redefining themselves and seem to be almost merging into each other. So the clear delineation between marketing, finance, engineering, production and logistics is becoming ever more blurred.

In addition, geographies too are blurring as every organisation has the ability to plunder the globe in search of customers. The worldwide web put paid to any ideas that we were not living in a global economy. I have friends who export English jams to the world, sell Danish furniture to the world and others who have in just two years built a million-dollar-business from Texas, founded entirely on a single barbecue sauce recipe! Interestingly enough, all these people previously had 'real jobs': another warning signal to consider. However, what this really means is that competitors can spring up anywhere these days, and because so many jobs are transferable (IT, product and project managers, HR etc) we need to take a very close look at what is happening around us.

It gets worse. Open access – due largely to data protection and freedom of information laws – means there is a lot more information available about our employees than ever before. Spend a few hours in the research department of a headhunter and you will be amazed at just how much data there is out there. A lot of that data is on-line, just sitting waiting for you to tap into it. This means that our employees are far more vulnerable than we might think. And, on top of that, smart recruiters can really play up to the 'be myself at work' mantra of the new-age employee. 'What a really cool lifestyle/workstyle opportunity, come and work with us.' A lot of us are going to be really up against it in the coming years, unless we change the way our employment offer is presented and fulfilled.

The talent officer in your business

I made it clear in Chapter 7 that one of HR's responsibilities is the search for talent inside and outside the organisation. In terms of what happens next, the appointment of talent officers has to be on the list. We cannot afford not to have someone in this role, whose job is to discover talent for the business and also uncover hidden talent inside. Good talent managers are a net gain to the organisation in both money and time. By knowing where to look, they save recruiting time. By knowing who is ready to 'fly the coop', and preventing it by making sure they are re-engaged, they increase retention rates and thereby save on recruitment costs. You don't have to call them talent managers, but they are needed more than ever in today's complex world. The talent manager can also support, train and mentor those divisional or unit people managers, underscoring an organisation's commitment to employee excellence.

That is where I see the future emphasis being laid. All these things are critical and all of them will impact on the types of people we employ, or more importantly who choose to come and work with us.

Head-to-head with the CEO

So how do you get this onto the strategic agenda? How is life/work balance going to play out with the CEO and his team?

So how do you get this on to the strategic agenda? How is life/work balance going to play out with the CEO and his team?

That, I suppose, depends to begin with just where you figure in the organisational pecking order. Are you really on the top team (a member of the management board) or are you a level below?

This positioning is crucial because, of course, the position of HR in any firm speaks volumes about just how well regarded (and how likely to be listened to) is the function.

Quite frankly, my own view on this is that unless you have a direct relationship with the CEO – and hopefully are a member of the strategic management group – you are possibly going to have a really hard time making much headway on this whole lifestyle/workstyle issue. Reason? Your work colleagues don't think enough about the people issues to accord it the right level of respect in the decision-making process.

So, with the exception of the following paragraph, I am going to assume that you have access and your voice is listened to in most cases. And that is what most of this part is about.

Go grab a champion

If, unfortunately, you are one of those people who hasn't really got the ear of the CEO and the rest of the top management team, don't despair. The option open to you is to find a champion – a member of the top management group that you respect – and persuade them to take the message about changing demographics and desires to the managing board for you. Of course, this is a second-class option, but it is better than nothing. And it will get you recognition. Without a champion you won't get very far, but then neither will the business. Lifestyle/workstyle employees vote with their hearts and then their feet. They know what they want and they increasingly know where to get it, especially in an economy where options are opening daily.

Count the cost and scare them too

If, however, you are a confidant of the CEO and the rest of the top management team then don't hold back. By the way, many senior managers over the years have told me that they rely on their HR director to keep the CEO in line, and manage him or her when it comes to any organisational issues. Therefore there is no reason to hold back.

My thought, based on what HR professionals and external experts have told me, is that this is a three-phase attack:

- Phase one: count the cost and scare them.
- Phase two: make the case for change.
- Phase three: reinforce the message from the outside.

Let's see how the attack might work.

Count the cost and scare them

People issues may be considered 'soft' by some. This is *not* a soft issue. It has its roots in the success or failure of the business by its ability or inability to attract and retain the right people. Therefore, it is initially a strategic issue. If you don't tackle it properly, you will have failed in your job as the people person in your firm.

Some years ago, I was lucky enough to meet a woman called Nancy Cravsin McClain, the then head of HR at Abbott Laboratories. Headquartered outside Chicago, they thought they understood a lot about talent. That was until Nancy Cravsin McClain told them the bits they'd been missing. Tired of trying to get people on to the agenda, she did an audit and put 'bounties' on the heads of the top 200 plus people in the firm.

Then she got on to the CEO's radar screen and showed him how much it would cost the company if these people left. The effect was staggering. People issues, recruitment and retention issues moved rapidly up the strategic agenda.

this is what any HR professional needs to do. For part of your time, stop thinking people and think numbers

And this is what any HR professional needs to do. For part of your time, stop thinking people and think numbers (I have already stressed this). CEOs, CFOs, CMOs and so on, don't just like numbers they *live* them. Join their game (stop trying to make up your own game, they won't want to come out and play). Show them numbers reflecting what happens if:

- They lose critical members of staff (in lost business, contacts, experience, credibility and cost of rehiring).
- They lose critical teams of staff (in lost business, contacts, experience, credibility, opportunity and cost of rehiring).
- They fail to recognise that people want a different deal than the one they've been working with (the cost of effective talent and people management versus the likely costs of 'voluntary attrition').
- They don't have a real succession policy (not a 'plan', but a real succession policy that managers are judged and rewarded by meeting).

You do the engagement audit (involve a couple of other top managers in the initial processes if you can), you add up the figures. Then take the Horror Show to the boardroom.

Calculating the cost

If your organisation has a sales team look at how much more the top 10 per cent of your sales reps bring in compared to the average of the bottom 90%. That's the average that losing those people will cost you – but only part of it. That's the average that you'll be down once their replacement is up and running. How long will that take? Track how long an average sales rep takes before they are bringing in an average level of sales (two months, three, six, a year?) Calculate what your star performer would have delivered during the same time. Finally try to work out the cost if your top sales people took some of your customers with them to a competitor – remember your customers may be more loyal to your sales rep than to your company.

Alternatively, look at your IT systems. If you are like most organisations you probably have a few pieces of out-dated legacy software that make doing some simple things very complicated. Somewhere in your organisation there is a, probably low-ranking, long-time employee who knows all the shortcuts, who knows how to get things done. He or she is the person that others go to, to find out how to work around the beast. They may only be paid £10,000 a year but they are providing IT consultancy that would cost you £100 an hour if they left. You need to know who that person is.

If you have done your maths homework correctly, you will get their attention. And you should get action. Lots of it.

But you are not finished. What has to happen now is reinforcement. And that comes in two ways.

One: making the case for change

Once you have run the numbers and got the attention of the top management group it is time to present the real facts. Assuming they recognise clearly the argument that it is going to be very costly not to be worried about employee engagement in the future, move along to the next phase and make the case for change.

Now you have them worried, you have them concerned. You have their attention.

Now is the time to explain – without turning it into a sociology lecture – how the employment mix and its desires and expectations are changing. How, if we want to engage our employees and get the very best out of them, we must be certain that they can get the very best out of us.

To do that, you need to explain the changes in the make up of your employees. Explain the lifestyle/workstyle options that people expect. Explain the need for flexibility. Again, though, put the numbers down. Illustrate what it means if you carry out the changes and successfully retain a significant portion of the workforce by setting some simple things in place to enhance their engagement quotient.

It boils down to this. In phase 1 you scared them by the costs of people leaving (in lost business and recruiting terms). In phase 2 you showed how much you can save when people choose to stay (how managing employee engagement impacts the bottom line).

But you still are not finished. What you need is confirmation.

Two: endorsement of your needs for change

The best way to do this is find a fellow believer inside (top management is the place to look) and then quickly move to reinforce your views from the outside. It is a very strange thing, but most CEOs like to open a door, just occasionally of course, to the outside world. It makes them feel in touch with reality (even if that 'reality' is in the shape of a $10,000 a day consultant).

Suggesting external confirmation of the changes that are taking place, the vulnerability of the workforce and the need to alter how you manage the employer/employee contract will, most likely, be agreed to with alacrity.

I would attempt to achieve this by first involving one or two external business commentators and researchers (possibly in presentations and discussion with the managing board). From there I would push hard to have the lifestyle/workstyle equation and how to manage the engagement process as the centrepiece – the theme – of your next management meeting: even better if you can get the top 50, 100 or 200 managers singing the same tune and hearing the same concerns (in numbers as well please!).

All this will build momentum, the theory will take on a life of its own and become part of what the business does. The concept of employees who are themselves at work, who bring who they are to work and want a lifestyle/workstyle pattern can then be embraced. The best way to do this is to develop an 'engagement index' that regularly (every six months is good) 'polls' employees on their attitudes to work, allowing you to track their levels of commitment.

Obviously, more is involved. It takes energy to sustain the concept, it takes time and, yes, it takes some money. But most of all it takes a change in attitude.

The rules of engagement have changed. Help your business to recognise that and then do something practical about it.

KEY ISSUES

- You need real people managers, not just executives with 'manager' on their business card.
- Create people managers whose job is to make sure the 'techies' in your business get their needs and expectations fully met.
- Expect to hire teams of talent, not just individuals. This is a trend just getting underway again.
- Talent agents (currently masquerading as interim management operators) are beginning to develop, and business loves them as they give huge flexibility.
- Expect to share talent with other firms, particularly joint-ventures and alliances.
- A need to be able to manage people not on your direct payroll will call for negotiation and persuasion skills.
- The need for an over-50 strategy, to make best use of this generation and make sure they don't block the pipeline for upcoming talent.
- A need for a diversity plan to get new people with new skills into the business.
- The need to create the 'cosy' workplace where employees feel they do contribute and are not just part of a huge corporate machine.
- Be ready for unknown competitors as job responsibilities merge and technology makes every business global.
- Appoint a talent officer to care about finding the best outside AND inside your business.
- Learn how to 'sell' these emerging people issues to the CEO and top management.
- Get help from outside to confirm what's happening and get the CEO's attention.
- Work at getting the top managers from around the firm 'on-side' to the workplace revolution.

Conclusion

Hopefully we now all realise that our employees are demanding and receiving a working deal based on flexibility and freedom. For those who have long predicted a new world of work we now have exactly that: a lifestyle/workstyle world where we all have our own private portfolio of tasks to be accomplished and we complete them in any way we choose, as long as we do deliver.

If your business wants to be seen as a talent magnet you are going to have to build this ability to be naturally flexible into your operational culture. And it must be effected practically subconsciously – it must come naturally to the business.

Let's recap on some of the key trends that are shaping employee expectations of the business they work with, and the challenges that companies who want to hire and hold talent are going to have to meet.

The niche workplace

People are already seeking out workplaces and individual jobs that match their values, expectations, personality and lifestyle/workstyle. Today, there is a broader range than ever to choose from. If you are a high-tech, cool customer, you'll go for a start-up where you can play video games in your downtime. If you are creative, you'll head for a new media organisation in New York or London's Soho. If you are the caring kind, you'll go to a global charity or not-for-profit organisation. Organisations are already turning on the talent magnet by differentiating themselves from others – and letting people know what they stand for, what their values are. Others are, frankly, losing out. So there is a huge need for many to play catch-up. Why? Well it would appear that some organisations (although still in the minority) are getting really good at understanding and embracing the lifestyle/workstyle trend.

Watch out for employer of choice battles

This horrible phrase (already clogging up the chairman's statement in far too many annual reports) is set, sadly, to get top billing in the business lexicons. Wanting to be an employer of choice usually means you have a problem and need to fix it – FAST. Those that really are employers of choice – unless they are incredibly smug – don't talk about it, they just are. However, real-life employers of choice (wherever in the world they are) do have several things in common that we would do well to recognise:

- A recognised and organised formal life/work balance programme that meets needs across the business.
- Professional and personal development opportunities for all.
- The ability to make a contribution to the firm tied to personal responsibility.
- A friendly and culturally rich environment ('being with others I can relate to'), that nurtures and then maximises potential.
- A business that is responsible to the community as a whole (this plays strongly to the lifestyle/workstyle employees' need to contribute to more than just a job).

The 'I'm-best-at-being-me' syndrome

We all used to talk about personal responsibility and the chance to make a contribution – now it's a reality. Increasingly employees at all levels want to be themselves. The 'I-am-the-best-at-being-me' mantra will manifest itself increasingly as employees demand that their workplace fully recognises their needs and expectations. Studies on both

employees at all levels (from senior managers to office juniors) increasingly list the need for 'personal authenticity' among their key criteria for job satisfaction.

sides of the Atlantic suggest that employees at all levels (from senior managers to office juniors) increasingly list the need for 'personal authenticity' among their key criteria for job satisfaction. It is no longer enough to meet the needs for a challenge or a good salary; we must also allow people to 'be themselves at work.'

Walk the talk or we walk out

The changing profile, demands and expectations of employees, coupled with an increasing shortage of talent, will put huge pressures on managers. Knowing they have control, employees will take an increasingly activist stance and demand that their worth be recognised. And this will happen across the board from a newly minted MBA to a 50-year-old middle manager who wants to work part-time. If we don't recognise these undercurrents already stirring in our firms – and make sure that our management from the top down reacts accordingly – we are going to reduce seriously our talent choices and we will quickly witness the departure of key workers.

Let's be ethical too

In the beginning it was tobacco and arms manufacturers, today it is oil, auto and transport companies. The companies who have their work cut out to attract groups in society who see their way of doing business as something unethical. Again, this reduces the recruitment and retention options of certain companies still further.

Just not sexy enough

A lot of employers are going to have to realise that whatever they peddle in goods and services is not a turn on. Already – as we have mentioned earlier – employees want to work with recognised names, brands and those that are leaders in the business. Conversely they are turned off industries that appear boring, grey and just plain unexciting. While this may smell like an opportunity for advertising and public relations agencies to do their stuff, it is in fact a huge job for corporate recruiters and HR professionals. We are going to have to sharpen up the image of many of our dowdy old firms if we are to attract those who run their lives in a lifestyle/workstyle fashion.

A new renaissance?

Work will become just a part of what we do and who we are. Our lives will become a cycle of, work, further education and personal pursuits. There will be no official finish line based on age. Some people will 'retire' early while others will work on for either fun or financial reasons.

Now how would this pattern of work, education and personal pursuits play in your business? These ideas are no longer 'out-of-the-box' but very much part of a growing day-to-day reality. If we want to capture talent, and more importantly get it to turn up on our doorstep each and every day, we need to consider them. And you need to get them on to that strategic business agenda.

There are – it has to be said – companies that 'get this' new wave of need. Sara Lee's operations in Australia have a work contract that actually says, 'There are no fixed hours. We don't care when people come to work as long as they achieve what we agree their work responsibilities are.' In the UK, Dutton Engineering has introduced a working year. Employees work a fixed number of hours per year, with the plan that they increase their presence when things get really busy. In Belgium, the printing firm Casterman has a working week that lasts only a weekend Friday night to Sunday night plus one full Friday every fortnight. There's a queue to volunteer.

Start thinking of maximising minorities

We are still not using the minorities in our societies very well. I have mentioned this before and make no apology for the repetition.

- **Immigrants:** while the US tries ever harder, most of Europe stumbles. Countries like the UK, France, Germany, Belgium and Holland all have large immigrant minorities who still do not make it, even after three generations, into mainstream business. Many of them become increasingly angry at being disenfranchised because few ever break through the glass ceiling that prevents their integration. If you as a business cannot contemplate the idea of a major change in the racial and religious mix of your workforce, you will have a problem – it's called being starved of talent. In a few more years we will need to draw more and more talent from emerging markets. Talent, for example, that is rooted in Buddhist, Muslim and Hindu cultures. How are we going to make that stick? How indeed? Most organisations don't even know how to start that discussion, but they are going to have to do so. Without it you will not only starve the bottom end of your business, but you will have no experts or new managers either. Being a talent magnet isn't about being glitzy and perceived to be a great place to work ... it's about knowing what is really happening out there in the real world and capitalising on it in the best way you can.
- **The socially disadvantaged:** technology brings the opportunity for many long-term unemployed, out-of-work single mothers and the handicapped to do meaningful work that removes them from welfare dependence. Companies need to think this through more imaginatively. An example might be to enable a single mother to be an 'at-

home' call centre, fielding enquiries from customers in another time zone when her children are in bed. Simple, inexpensive technology enables this type of option, creating a new talent pool.

- **Sandwiched employees:** our caring society has created a major problem that few are fully aware of – people live longer and longer and longer. Because of this, many employees find themselves with the double whammy of dealing with both childcare and eldercare; sandwiching employees in a vice that creates stress and causes major money worries. Corporations have to recognise this (in some countries the figure for 'sandwiched' employees in the workforce is put at 20 per cent and rising) and have flexible systems that can help employees either cope or find alternative options. Failure to do this puts a lot of unhappy talent on the market that will happily work for someone who can help to solve or alleviate these problems.

- **Women:** in many countries and industries, women are still not recognised as key players in business and some wonder if they ever will be. The fallout from the major corporations (often due to frustration at the lack of recognition or opportunity) shows little sign of abating. Industries like oil and gas, engineering, transport and financial services are, in the main, still boys' clubs. But if you want to be a talent magnet is it to be a 'men only' magnet, and can you afford for that to happen? And just in case we delude ourselves into thinking that the women in management initiative is going anywhere soon, let's remember that less than 1 per cent of executive directors in the US are female. But we are running out of options, and it may be time to change that. Although I think I first wrote that last sentence about 20 years ago!

Get ready for a rush of retirees

Again, too few senior executives have really thought through or even begun to admit just how much talent is on the brink of departure. This is strange, because in many cases it includes themselves! Some companies in the US claim to be facing the loss of up to 60 per cent of their executive talent pool over the next three to five years as the 55s and over take the money and run to the country club (not surprising when nearly half of the US workforce is nearly 50 or over). The story is the same in Europe and Japan. The biggest concern here is that there are few replacements due to the downsizing of the early 1990s. So companies have to turn on that talent magnet just to get these people to stay – even for a few valuable hours each week. Savvy managers say that they are already putting highly flexible, and lucrative offers in place that include:

- part-time assignments
- mentoring roles
- telecommuting (cross state/cross-border)
- shared jobs
- variable pay, based on time worked and goals met.

Reputation

To conclude, my view is that, perhaps after all, reputation – or more accurately, perceived reputation – may well be what certainly attracts, and may then help to hold people. But don't be too complacent. Life today is fast and furious. A bad reputation today leads to a good reputation tomorrow. For example: Company A throws out 10,000 people and the analysts applaud and the would-be worker eventually beats a path to their door. Why? Because the stock looks good, opportunities look good (they are lean and mean) and they have swept away all the dead wood, allowing people to, wait for it, 'be themselves at work.' The fact that this is the only way they can recruit people is irrelevant. Why? Because this is the new way of doing business.

And there is something everyone needs to keep in their heads. We can't keep people for very long – I don't mean forever, or for 20 years (which we don't want to anyway), but even for a couple of years – unless we learn to play the new game and learn the new rules (which, annoyingly, get re-invented every time you play the game). Maybe what we should be considering is that our success – our ability to hire in talent – will be based on one thing: that we can hire people faster and hold people longer than our competitors. Why? Because we do all the things that our employees demand. Could that be the new success factor?

What we need to realise, and soon, is that corporate popularity is ephemeral. We write off organisations only to see them rise again from the ashes. Conversely, we gave huge plaudits to businesses that never, ever deserved it.

- We will have shorter spans of being popular as businesses. The longer we can hang in the better though, so we need to find better ways to manage that process and shorten the downtime between industry darling and industry dunce.

- Going down faster means we can come back quicker if we get the next business wave right.

- Perception management will grow: managing the corporate reputation needs big bucks thrown at it and needs to change its message constantly to attract the right kind of people.

Don't look for long-stay talent, learn to manage a fluid workforce: employees who may well have three or four mini-'careers'

- Don't look for long-stay talent, learn to manage a fluid workforce: employees who may well have three or four mini-'careers' in your business at different times of their lifestyle/workstyle existence.
- That somewhat bizarre idea, employee branding, is consigned to where it should be – the garbage can. You can brand your business, your products, your service, but not your people. They belong to themselves, not you. Remember they want to be THEMSELVES at work– their lifestyle/workstyle demands it. Advice: don't stick labels on talent, they don't really want it and they won't thank you for it. If they feel good about your business they'll let you know and they'll tell others on their own terms – not yours.

What I really, really want

As I began this book, I pointed out that there were – if we really bothered to sit down and think it through – a remarkable number of things that individuals and organisations have in common.

Researching and writing this book hasn't changed my mind at all. More than ever I can see that the whole basis of lifestyle/workstyle has been gradually evolving over a long period of time. It has its roots in how we as corporations have treated individuals. Even – let it be said – how we ourselves have been treated by those we have worked for.

What we need to do now is begin to manage those expectations, those synergies that make employer and employee click. If we can get our managers to understand how to manage employees with these needs we will be well on our way to creating the true new-age business. More than ever, with every day that passes, I see examples of what Mr and Ms Average employee of the twenty-first century are seeking. And, tragically in some cases, I see corporations unable to adapt and bend to new ways of working, new ways of rewarding, new ways of retaining people. But there are so many things that individuals and organisations have in common that it seems ludicrous they can't get this modern 'marriage' right.

Just look again and consider: how do I make my business work to meet these needs? It can't be that difficult. Can it? If 'us' and 'them' essentially want the same things, can't we work together in some kind of harmony? This little chart is on my wall and I look at it every day to remind myself. Better still, cut it out and read it on the way to work. I guarantee that if you memorise the points on this chart, you'll have a whole different attitude to this new-age work contract debate.

Table 3
WHAT PEOPLE AND ORGANISATIONS WANT

People Want To	Organisations Want To
• Enjoy life and work, achieve success and excel at what they do	• Engage the people they serve and enable, encourage and reward outstanding performance
• Do work they care about on their own terms; create and deliver financial and human value	• Provide enriching products and services; create and deliver financial and human value to all the stakeholders they interact with
• Create and express a unique professional identity as 'themselves'	• Create and build a distinctive corporate brand
• Find the right organisation and the role that suits them best	• Find the best people and match them to the right roles
• Use their skills, stretch themselves and develop new abilities in their personal and professional lives	• Use the skills of their people, improve effectiveness and drive value growth
• Make a valued and recognised contribution to organisations who understand their lifestyle/ workstyle needs	• Enable and reward contribution to corporate purpose

Index

Free chapter

If you have enjoyed *The New Rules of Engagement* you'll probably be interested in *Becoming an Employer of Choice: Make your organisation a place where people want to do great work* by Judith Leary-Joyce. To whet your appetite we have included the first chapter of this best-selling book free. You can order a copy of the book by visiting www.cipd.co.uk/bookstore.

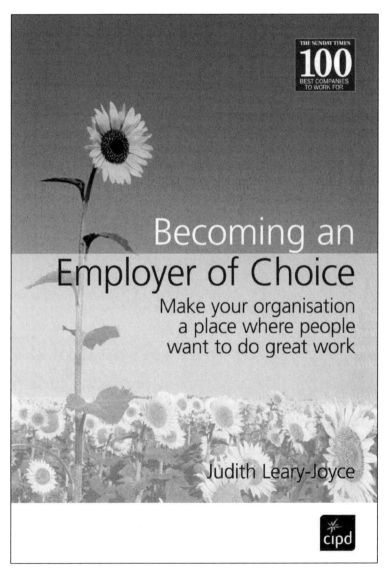

A free sample chapter from *Becoming an Employer of Choice*

Chapter 1

The business case

This chapter could consist of just one statement:

> Great companies consistently outperform the FTSE All Share. Over the past five years the best companies would have earned an investor a compounded annual return of 12.1 per cent, compared with a 5.8 per cent decline in the FTSE All Share index as a whole.
>
> Source: Sunday Times 100 Best Companies to Work For list, 2003
> Statistics by Frank Russell Company

How interested would your shareholders be in your corporate culture if they knew that? They would really want you to become an employer of choice because it is good for the bottom line.

It is a universal truth of business that no matter how unique or innovative your products and systems are, it is only a matter of time before someone else is doing it as well or better than you. If you are a market leader, you have to keep running hard to stay ahead of the hounds snapping at your heels, and if you are one of the chasing pack, you will get breathless just keeping up.

The only thing your competitors cannot copy – your only truly unique and lasting competitive edge – is your people. That familiar rhetoric of the annual report is true: your people really are your greatest asset. Or they will be, if you build a work environment in which they can shine.

It is not worth worrying that others might pinch your ideas and products – they definitely will, alongside undercutting your price. Better to utilise your people to the full and go right on leading the field, while they struggle to keep up. But how to do that? This book is full of thoughts and ideas from those named as Great Companies. And the facts below and in the draft presentation in Appendix 3 give you even more reason to read on.

1

A free sample chapter from *Becoming an Employer of Choice*

2   BECOMING AN EMPLOYER OF CHOICE

The Facts

In short, great company culture will give you:

• easy recruitment
• powerful retention
• high levels of creativity and innovation
• improved customer service
• a great workplace that customers like too.

Easy recruitment

Once people hear what an exciting workplace you have, they will flock to join you. Those companies that made it into the *Sunday Times 100 Best Companies to Work For* list have proved this in spades. Timpson is a perfect example of this.

In 2001, prior to the publication of the *50 Best Companies to Work For* list, Timpson had 80 per cent employment. After publication this increased to 100 per cent. And by 2002, when named again as one of the *100 Best Companies to Work For*, Timpson had a waiting list and was attracting women and graduates for the first time. The end result is a jump in profits from £3 million in 2001 to £6.5 million in 2003.

Such is the power of great company culture – energetic, dynamic people want to work with you, knowing they will enjoy their work and develop their career into the bargain. The business can choose the best person for the job, providing the very best option for success.

Powerful retention

Once people realise they are in a good workplace, they want to stay. Great companies develop careers in house – growing their own to make sure they keep all the expertise and experience. They also involve colleagues in seeking the best way to run the business, listening to their ideas and concerns from the front line. What young high-potential person can resist that? From the moment they walk through the door, management are paying attention, listening well and looking to three jobs down the line – it is a compelling argument for commitment. Especially when linked to a challenging and honest workplace.

Claridges demonstrate this well. They instigated a major culture change, including consulting colleagues on what changes were necessary in the business, and daily staff briefings. The end result was that staff turnover reduced from 73 per cent to 16 per cent in five years.

A free sample chapter from *Becoming an Employer of Choice*

Imagine the bottom-line impact when recruitment costs fall and less time is lost as the outgoing person shifts his or her attention away from the work and the incoming arrival strives to grasp the intricacies of a new job.

High levels of creativity and innovation

Provide challenge and support in appropriate balance and you will stimulate the creative juices. Couple this with a strong feeling of belonging so that people speak of the workplace as 'their company' and 'like family' and you have a heady mix for any growing business. Everyone in the organisation takes responsibility and focuses on what will serve the business best. People who feel an attachment to the community watch for pitfalls and have great ideas about how to deal with them.

Hiscox are a prime example. They were part of the syndicate that insured the World Trade Centre, so business took a major hit in 2001. Because their commitment to colleagues includes appreciating the wisdom of experience, they were able to ride the storm and bring the business to a better position within the year.

Improved customer service

The very best customer service operations have excellent people cultures. We can give only as much as we receive. Just like money: if we have it, we can enjoy spending it; when we are broke, we get depressed or borrow – which costs us dear in the long run. It is the same with customer relationships: people cannot give what they do not have, and if they try to give what is not real for them, it will cost everyone dear in the long run.

Take Flight Centre. Strong working relationships encourage colleagues to build equally strong relationships with customers, who then return to them time and again for help. The end result is 23 new shops and businesses opened in 2002, giving a jump in turnover of 36 per cent, leading to a 100 per cent increase in profits.

People who feel cared for, respected and valued give high-quality customer service, building loyal and committed relationships that are more effective than the very best marketing and PR.

Customers like great workplaces

In this day and age, ethics in business has a high profile. People will take their custom away from organisations that do not live up to

A free sample chapter from *Becoming an Employer of Choice*

expected standards, so being known as a great workplace will help differentiate you from competitors. When faced with a choice of provider, people are more likely to go for the company that is known as a fantastic employer. Supporting an organisation that exploits colleagues is not a good option.

TD Industries are known for high trust and integrity by partners (employees), suppliers and customers. To quote Jack Lowe Jnr, the CEO:

> I am convinced that high trust has allowed us to be agile and aggressive during these difficult economic times and continue to outperform our industry. TD always emerges from difficult times with a strengthened position in our marketplace.

To test his judgement on this, look at the graph on slide number 9 in the business case/evidence (Appendix 3) – it speaks volumes.

More facts
Low trust costs you money
People will concentrate on looking after themselves if they do not trust the organisation. This leads to higher costs as they cover their backs and take the safest options on suppliers, etc. When trust is high, people look for the best options, build strong supplier relationships and costs go down.

See the research findings on slide 7 of Appendix 3.

Retention figures drop
Each new recruit costs you twice the annual salary. See your retention figures improve by 10 to 20 per cent and you are making a real saving to the bottom line.

See the figures on slide 5 of Appendix 3, and compare those of your sector.

Recruitment becomes easier
Once yours is known as a great workplace, people want to join and their applications increase. When people love their work, they talk about it and encourage suitable people to apply for a job – so some of the vetting will have been done for you.

See the recruitment results on slide 20 of Appendix 3.

A free sample chapter from *Becoming an Employer of Choice*

Leadership affects the bottom line

Sound leadership respects people and provides them with the environment in which they can do their best work. Holding the power lightly and sharing responsibility makes the best of talent and impacts directly on the results of the business.

See the results of TD Industries once they instigated Servant Leadership – slide 9 of Appendix 3.

What gets measured gets done

Great companies set clear measures, then reward and celebrate success. People feel valued and see the benefits of doing a great job. Whether rewards are financial or through public appreciation, the results impact on the bottom line.

See the achievements of Flight Centre, slide 13 of Appendix 3.

Two-way communication is a business necessity

Giving information from the top is generally accepted; receiving it from below is often forgotten. Two-way communication ensures buy-in and commitment to the company, which pays off in direct improvement in performance.

See the Claridges results from a culture change, slide 23 of Appendix 3.

Conclusion

It may not be easy, but it is worth it. Great companies benefit in numerous ways – many that cannot be quantified. But the bottom line figures speak for themselves.

Even when you are an employer of choice, there will be difficult times: you will be prone to the same vagaries of the market as every other company. But do expect your people to pull out all the stops to give the company the best possible chance, and to stay loyal through the toughest of times. Care for them well at all times and they will return the favour tenfold.